THE BIOGRAPHY

RYAN GOSLING

HOLLYWOOD'S FINEST

THE BIOGRAPHY

RYAN GOSLING

HOLLYWOOD'S FINEST

NICK JOHNSTONE

JOHN BLAKE

Published by John Blake Publishing Ltd,
3 Bramber Court, 2 Bramber Road,
London W14 9PB, England

www.johnblakepublishing.co.uk

www.facebook.com/Johnblakepub   facebook

twitter.com/johnblakepub   twitter

This edition published in 2013

ISBN: 978 1 78219 460 6

British Library Cataloguing-in-Publication Data:

A catalogue record for this book is available from the British Library.

Design by www.envydesign.co.uk

Printed and bound in Great Britain by CPI Group (UK) Ltd

1 3 5 7 9 10 8 6 4 2

© Text copyright Nick Johnstone 2013

Papers used by John Blake Publishing are natural, recyclable
products made from wood grown in sustainable forests.
The manufacturing processes conform to the
environmental regulations of the country of origin.

Every attempt has been made to contact the relevant copyright-holders,
but some were unobtainable. We would be grateful if
the appropriate people could contact us.

The author would like to make clear that the subject of the book, Ryan Gosling, has in no way participated with the writing of this book.

CONTENTS

HOLLYWOOD'S FINEST

Ryan Gosling's story is not the story of an actor born into a privileged Hollywood family, whose parents were producers, screenwriters, publicists, directors, cinematographers or talent agents. Instead, it's the remarkable tale of a small-city Canadian boy from a modest background, who, through hard work, perseverance, the occasional lucky break and a bright, shining talent, has managed to turn himself into one of the most respected actors of his generation.

In 1993, when Ryan was 12, he first came to attention as a Mouseketeer on the then latest incarnation of Disney's long-standing children's TV show, *The All New Mickey Mouse Club*. He got the lucky break after beating 15,000 other hopefuls at auditions that started in Montreal and moved down to Florida, where Disney would film the show. Hired for his singing and dancing potential, Ryan became one of Canada's rare Mouseketeers.

On the show, the softly spoken, floppy fringed Ryan appeared alongside a cluster of firecracker talents who would all go quickly on to become adored and screamed-over pop stars: Britney Spears, Justin Timberlake and Christina Aguilera. Witnessing their passion and talent on a daily basis and how it would likely lead them to careers as pop stars, singers or professional dancers, Ryan had a sinking feeling because he knew that none of that trio of professional directions in life was calling out to him with the same sparkling appeal that it was to his Mouseketeer peers.

When Disney wound up the show's latest run at the end of Season 7 in 1994 due to ailing ratings, Ryan's lucky break came to a sudden end. Ryan, who had been living with fellow Mouseketeer Justin Timberlake and his family, so his mother could work back at home, now moved back in with his mother and sister in Canada. Although he found high school tolerable, it hardly matched the showbiz life he'd been living. Deciding his future lay in acting, not singing and dancing, he worked hard, focusing his energies on using his *Mickey Mouse Club* break and experience to gain a foot in the door in the world of TV. In no time, his mother was ferrying him to auditions, and he was landing small one-off parts in TV shows. Through-out high school, he won part after TV part, each one more significant than its predecessor.

While the TV work came to him often enough that he was able to build up an impressive list of credits for himself, Ryan felt that the work wasn't satisfying him in the way that he wanted. This feeling persisted, even after he landed the recurring role of Sean Hanlon across 1997–98 – which meant a lengthy commitment and, with it, financial security – on high-profile Canadian teen show *Breaker High*. As had happened on *The All New Mickey Mouse Club*, he became increasingly convinced that acting for TV wasn't his destiny either: instead, he wanted to move up to film.

Once he had come to this decision, Ryan believed it was time to make the move to Los Angeles, so he could be near the mythical centre of the film industry and have the potential to audition for a more wide-reaching choice of roles. And so it was, age 17, that Ryan touched down in Los Angeles. Via help from his TV contacts, he quickly signed on with an agent.

Ryan's first big break in Los Angeles came in the form of the lead role of Hercules in a new TV series, *Young Hercules*, a spin-off of the hit TV show *Hercules: The Legendary Journeys*. For this historical adventure show, which would feature demanding physical work, Ryan needed to go straight into intensive training to get in shape.

This delighted him because it gave him the chance to prepare for the character he'd be playing, in the manner of his favourite actors – Marlon Brando, James Dean and Gary Oldman.

Young Hercules was filmed on location in New Zealand. Ryan flew out and was based there for the next six months. By the end of filming, he was once more disillusioned. Spending his days, as he would later say, cavorting around with 'a fake tan, leather pants, fighting imaginary monsters' just wasn't for him either. His sense of integrity, fuelled by adolescent leisure time spent devouring films by high-integrity directors such as David Lynch, made him even more convinced to walk away from his blossoming TV career and go flat out with a bid to move into film.

The move, which would head off the imminent day when he'd be cornered after having been typecast as a children's TV actor, proved to be a smart one. But the transition didn't happen overnight. After all, his résumé showcased a singing and dancing Mouseketeer-turned-children's-TV-actor – a background that didn't exactly set him up for the transition into the far more serious sphere of feature film.

Despite the obvious obstacles, Ryan got around them, and, through his agent sending him for auditions, he landed his first film break: a tiny role as a football player called Alan Bosley in *Remember The Titans*, a hit 2000 movie, starring Denzel Washington. Even with a small part, Ryan lit up the screen during a locker-room scene where, as his teammates sang along to soul classic 'Ain't No Mountain High Enough', he called on his dance background to steal the scene with his vivacious dancing. His abundant charisma, which had wowed Justin Timberlake when they were working together as Mouseketeers, was cut loose here and seemed uncontainable. Anyone watching the movie today can see how obviously hungry Ryan was to be noticed as a film actor, how much he wanted it, how magnetic his onscreen presence was, how utterly focused he was on making the leap from the locked genre of children's TV into the sea of possibility that was the reality of feature film-making.

His big break – and it was just as big in scale as being plucked out of 15,000 Canadian kids to become a Mouseketeer – came when he was 19 years old, when he landed the lead in an independent film called *The Believer* (2001), which would see him play a 'Jewish Nazi' – a conflicted, repugnant and complex character.

Stunned that he had landed the part, Ryan threw himself into intense, dedicated preparation, learning Hebrew and studying Judaism. In so doing, he demonstrated a total commitment to depicting his character as absolutely as possible. This complete immersion in a role has, of course, become a trademark of his acting work and explains why so many people assume he is following a Method acting approach – which he isn't; Ryan is somewhat remarkably untrained as an actor and completely self-taught.

Lending Ryan's bid to earn himself a reputation as a film actor overnight gravitas, *The Believer* won the Grand Jury Prize – Dramatic at the Sundance Film Festival of 2001 and earned Ryan rave reviews for a mesmerising performance reminiscent of those of equal intensity from heavyweights such as Robert De Niro, Harvey Keitel and Christopher Walken.

After a gentle, quiet performance as another football player in a small independent movie, *The Slaughter Rule* (2002), Hollywood came knocking and Ryan found himself acting opposite a major movie star, Sandra Bullock, in the thriller *Murder By Numbers* (2002) – his first big-budget film. Delivering a brooding, intense performance, he appears onscreen like an actor who knows he's got a serious foot in the door of the feature film world and is impatient to pass through to the big time. Though neither Ryan nor his co-star has ever discussed this in public, Ryan and Bullock allegedly became close while filming the movie in early 2001. A year after finishing work on the film, in 2002, when Ryan was 21 and Bullock, 37, they reportedly began a year-long romance.

Even though his star was in the ascendant, Ryan decided to attach himself only to roles he felt connected to, roles that excited him. It made sense, since, after that long stretch of TV work, he wanted to be challenged, to be tested, to immerse himself in a character he felt connected to and who he believed needed to be given a voice in cinema. It was for all of these reasons that he signed up to play an emotionally detached teenager who kills his girlfriend's autistic brother in *The United States Of Leland* (2003). In the film, he delivers an icy, detached performance, which bears the influence of another actor whose work he greatly admired: Gary Oldman.

By this point, Ryan was heading into another typecasting scenario, only now, instead of being typecast as a children's TV actor, he was on the brink of being typecast as an actor who specialised in playing intense, out-there, brooding characters. To challenge and undo that reputation, he signed up next for the star-crossed lovers' epic *The Notebook* (2004), in which he would play Noah, a boy from the wrong side of the tracks, who falls for a Southern belle from a wealthy family.

Right after making *The Notebook*, as if to level out his sense of where his career was heading, he reverted to his former reputation for playing intense, troubled characters and took on another Gary Oldman-esque role in *Stay* (2005), a film in which he played a suicidal young man. If that part seemed to be steering him back into the intense corner, any such typecasting was blown out of the water with the release of *The Notebook*.

At first, the film opened gently, before starting to gain momentum, as audiences who reached the end credits in floods of tears turned it into a worldwide word-of-mouth hit. With its snowballing success, the media started to ramp up its focus on Ryan, pronouncing him – as channelled through his performance in *The Notebook* as Noah – a newly discovered Hollywood hunk, a pin-up, a dreamboat and so forth.

Ryan himself was somewhat taken by surprise at his new sex-symbol status and felt confused, since it seemed to detract from the seriousness of the work he was doing. He wanted to be noticed for his acting, not his looks. But that's an old Hollywood complaint, one that stretches back through the entire history of cinema, whereby actors and actresses have always resented being lauded for their perceived good looks as opposed to their talent for acting.

Adding to *The Notebook*'s runaway success, as had seemingly happened between Ryan and Sandra Bullock after making *Murder By Numbers*, Ryan and his *Notebook* co-star Canadian actress, Rachel McAdams, two years Ryan's senior – and, in a funny coincidence, also born in London, Ontario – began dating a year after *The Notebook* shoot wrapped. They would be together for the next two years. The mere notion that the stars of a romantic epic as sweeping as *The Notebook* had fallen in love in real life too proved irresistible to audiences, who set about scrutinising the film in search of moments, clues or evidence of a budding real-life chemistry between Ryan and McAdams as their onscreen characters fall madly in love.

To deal with this overnight mainstream attention and

success, which catapulted the 24-year-old to a completely different level as an actor, Ryan surprisingly broke his full-throttle sprint towards greater and bigger success in stepping out of acting altogether and taking – of all things – a job in a Los Angeles sandwich bar. He has mentioned this intriguing-sounding sabbatical from acting twice, once in an interview with *GQ*, telling the magazine of his sandwich-making prowess: 'People used to come in and request me.' The other time he has talked about it was in an interview with the *Guardian*, who called the sandwich shop a 'corner shop'. Speaking with the *Guardian*, Ryan explained how the job came about: 'I'd become friends with the guy who ran the shop, and he left me to watch it one day. I made some pretty goddamn good sandwiches and people wanted me to make them from then on, not him. I liked that job, but he fired me. He found out I was overcharging people that I knew had gotten stuff for free from him.'

Although social media was either in its infancy at this time (Facebook, YouTube) or not yet born (Twitter), celebrity news already travelled fast across the web and it seems fairly hard to comprehend how Ryan, even though he was yet to be a highly visible actor, was able to get away with working in a Los Angeles sandwich shop, without a single person – especially co-workers or regulars – recognising him from his TV or film work. However, based on what he told *GQ* and the *Guardian*, he managed to do it while remaining utterly incognito.

Sticking with the food theme, Ryan's sandwich-making sabbatical shifted to his co-founding, renovating and opening

Tagine, a Moroccan restaurant in Beverly Hills, in partnership with chef Ben Benameur and sommelier Chris Angulo. As Benameur explained the venture to *Lifestyle* magazine, 'He [Ryan] fell in love with my [Moroccan] food. I invited him to my place and he decided to open a business with me. From there, we never looked back.'

Ryan, who had become very interested in Africa – its people, their culture and the continent's politics – told Yahoo he poured much of the money he had amassed from his acting work to date into the venture: 'I bought it a few years ago on a whim. I was broke afterwards and had to do all the renovations by myself. Just alone to lay pipes took me half a year. In the meantime everything is done and I help as a waiter from time to time.'

If it seemed that his focus was moving away from acting, he brought it right back by beginning work on a trilogy of films. In each, he would deliver an unforgettable, off-the-cliff searing performance.

In *Half Nelson* (2006), which would earn him his first Academy Award nomination, Ryan played a drug-using high school teacher; in *Fracture* (2007), he played a Jelly Bean-chomping, hyperactive assistant district attorney eagerly trying to expose Anthony Hopkins' character's wrongdoing; and in *Lars And The Real Girl* (2007), arguably his most out-there role to date, he played a child-like, grief-stricken man whose only meaningful relationship in life is with a blow-up doll he lovingly names Bianca.

All three performances announced Ryan's new Brando-esque onscreen presence and the uncanny degree to which he brought each character to life onscreen via total immersion in the part.

What came next was an ill-fated stint in 2007, during which time Ryan was attached to Peter Jackson's adaptation of Alice Sebold's novel *The Lovely Bones*. As preparation to play the older character of Jack Salmon, Ryan gained 50lb and grew a straggly beard, a move which didn't chime at all with how the film's producers or director envisaged the character – leading to Ryan's withdrawing from the project shortly before filming started and being replaced by Mark Wahlberg.

Off *The Lovely Bones* project, Ryan found himself, as he put it, 'bald, fat and unemployed'. And so began another sabbatical of sorts. This time, instead of making sandwiches or co-founding a Moroccan restaurant (which, under the name of Tagine, had opened to positive reviews in 2006), he dedicated time to an eclectic band called Dead Man's Bones. He formed the group with Zach Shields, a fellow music-loving actor, whom he met because Shields happened to be dating Rachel McAdams' sister, Kayleen, at the same time as Ryan was dating Rachel. The two men developed a sound for their band and, during the three-year hiatus after his surprise departure from *The Lovely Bones* project, when Ryan would only commit himself to making two films, *All Good Things* (2010) and *Blue Valentine* (2010), they set about making and releasing an eponymously titled album of 'spooky doo-wop' music written to be performed as a duet with a children's choir and took it out on tour.

Ryan came out of that second sabbatical refreshed and ready to get back to acting. In the past few years, he has worked flat out, dashing from one project to the next. He delivered a barrage of charismatic, blistering performances in films as diverse as *Drive* (2011), *The Ides Of March* (2011), *Crazy, Stupid, Love* (2011), *The Place Beyond The Pines* (2012) and *The Gangster Squad* (2013), all of which have brought him further glowing reviews, award nominations and wins. They have also endowed him with a newfound status in which he's now unquestionably seen as one of the finest actors of his generation.

During this prolific period, when he has stopped going to premieres and awards ceremonies looking dressed down and unsure of how he felt about such industry get-togethers and, instead, turns up looking content, relaxed, confident and impeccably dressed, his legion of adoring female fans has grown ever larger, powered by the enduring conviction that the Ryan who appeared in *The Notebook* as Noah is the real Ryan and, hence, a man who would think nothing of building a house for the woman he loved and penning hundreds of devoted love letters, even if they didn't get a response.

His appeal in general, beyond his work in film, has also been fuelled by his eternal dedication to the woman in his life, notably his mother Donna and older sister Mandi (one or both of whom Ryan often proudly takes with him to high-profile events); by going most places with his beloved dog George; by reports that he's the kind of man who wades into a heated argument taking place on a New York street and thinks nothing of breaking it up and restoring peace; by his passionate going out to bat for social injustices, via associations with charities and NGOs, which has seen him make repeat visits to Africa with the Enough Project; by the fact that he co-fronts a band who write duets to sing with children's choirs dressed in spooky Halloween costume; by the fact that one of his favourite pastimes is to spend a day at Disneyland; by declarations in interviews that a perfect afternoon would involve a knitting session; by his ongoing taking of ballet classes; by the fact that he often seems shy and vulnerable; by his humble, charming demeanour – and by the fact that all of these aspects of his character have been mythologised by the many contagious blogs and memes sparked by the original, wildly influential single topic Tumblr, *Fuck Yeah! Ryan Gosling*. What's more, it's hard to think of many serious actors or actresses who have ever inspired the publication of a colouring book in their honour – something which happened to Ryan in 2012, when Mel Simone Elliott published her colouring-in book: *Colour Me Good, Ryan Gosling*.

All of which brings us to the present day, where Ryan is in a committed relationship with Eva Mendes, an actress six years his senior, whom he began dating, as per the pattern with Sandra Bullock and Rachel McAdams, shortly after finishing work acting opposite her in *The Place Beyond The Pines* (2012), in which the pair play an onscreen couple reunited by a shared love for their son.

Alongside further exciting films in the pipeline, including a second effort with *Drive* director Nicolas Winding Refn – *Only God Forgives* (2013) – and a starring role in a new Terrence Malick movie, Ryan has also now stepped over into the director's chair to make his directorial debut, with a film he has also written: *How To Catch A Monster*. Still only 32, his restless ambition appears to burn ever more fiercely. This is the remarkable story of how Ryan Gosling came to be one of Hollywood's finest actors.

CHAPTER ONE

A LITTLE PLACE CALLED LONDON

There's another lesser-known city in the world called London and it can be found in Ontario, Canada. Named after its sprawling British twin, London, England, it is located 195km west of the major Canadian city, Toronto. According to the most recent census information at the time of writing, London, Ontario has a population of just under 367,000.

It was in this London, on Wednesday, 12 November 1980, that Ryan Thomas Gosling was born to Thomas and Donna Gosling. That same day, the news was abuzz with fantastical tales of space travel, as the American space probe *Voyager 1* managed to send back pictures of its adventures orbiting Saturn.

Back on Planet Earth, Ryan was given his middle name after his father. He was not the couple's first child. Four years earlier, in 1976, Donna had given birth to a daughter, whom they named Mandi.

Ryan was born at St Joseph's Hospital, which can be found in London at 268 Grosvenor Street. It's known for being one of the oldest hospitals in the whole of Canada, having first opened in 1869.

The week Ryan was born, the most popular films of 1980 up to that point were *The Empire Strikes Back*, *Airplane!*, *Private Benjamin*, *Coal Miner's Daughter*, *Smokey And The Bandit II*, *The Blue Lagoon*, *The Blues Brothers*, *Ordinary People*, *Urban Cowboy* and *The Shining*, which gives you a sense of the cinematic climate he emerged into.

Born under the astrological sign of Scorpio, Ryan shares his birthday with melancholy-voiced Canadian singer/ songwriter Neil Young; as well as the chilling, incarcerated American cult leader Charles Manson, Romanian Olympic gymnast Nadia Comaneci, French sculptor Auguste Rodin, American actress and Princess of Monaco Grace Kelly, the French filmmaker Jacques Tourneur, who created works such as *Cat People* and *Days Of Glory*, and actress Anne Hathaway, star of such movies as *The Devil Wears Prada*, *Rachel Getting Married* and *One Day*.

At the time Ryan was born, his father – a descendant of French-Canadian lineage – would have been in his mid-twenties. Most reports state that Thomas Gosling worked as a travelling salesman for a paper mill when Ryan was a child. However, it's not clear if he was already doing this job when his son was born.

Ryan's mother, Donna, was a secretary during his early

years. Much later, according to *Radar online*, she would focus on her own study, graduating with a Bachelor of Arts in English from McMaster University in 2011 and then a Bachelor of Education from Brock University in 2012.

Back in November 1980, when the Goslings were tending to Ryan as a baby, London was still a relatively small city, with a population somewhere in the region of 250,000 people. Having been formally labelled the district of London in 1800, the area was declared a village in 1826. By 1855, commercial growth had seen the population swell to over 10,000 and, in response to that growth, there had been a round of legislative changes, which led to London becoming formally incorporated as a city.

That endorsement served as a catalyst for widespread growth, which kept the city expanding commercially and in terms of people moving there and setting up home, growing at a steady momentum, all the way until Ryan was born on that Wednesday in November 1980.

London wasn't to be his home for long though, and, when he was two years old, the family packed up and moved themselves to a new base in Cornwall, an even smaller city in Eastern Ontario. The move meant their new home was around 400 miles drive away from the home where Ryan had spent his baby years.

The relocation, and, with it, the universal sense of upheaval, came about because Ryan's father took a job working for a major paper mill in Cornwall called the Domtar Paper Mill. As mentioned earlier, it is unclear whether this was the job that saw Thomas Gosling become a travelling salesman for a paper mill or whether he had been doing the same job but for a different paper mill back in London. Regardless of which scenario it was, he would now settle into his role at Domtar Paper Mill and work for the firm for many years to come.

Cornwall sits on the banks of the St Lawrence River and its location connects it with the far larger cities of Ottawa, some 65 miles to the Northwest, and Montreal, around 71 miles to the Northeast. A recent census reveals in its data that approximately 70 per cent of those who live in the city speak English as their first language and that 24 per cent speak French as their first language – a dominating combination which gives Cornwall its distinct French- and English-speaking bilingual identity.

Due to its location making it a good defensive position, Cornwall was first established as a settlement back in 1784 by United Empire Loyalists who had migrated there from New York. With the support of the British government, they renamed what had earlier been called Pointe Maligne by French colonists New Johnstown. Then, in 1797, once it was firmly a part of the British colony of Upper Canada, New Johnstown was renamed for a third time as Cornwall, in honour of the Duke of Cornwall and the scenic, rugged coastal county of Cornwall, which lies in the southwest corner of England.

After that name change, Cornwall quickly grew to become a centre of industrial development and growth, as both paper and cotton mills were founded. As elsewhere across Canada, the opening of these new mills caused a population spike, as migrants heard about opportunities and flocked to the town in search of work. The influx meant that, by the end of the 19th century, the population had grown to the extent that it had surpassed 5,000 and many of the new inhabitants were French-Canadians.

Into the ongoing industrial boom, the Toronto Paper Company opened a mill in 1883, later renamed the Domtar Paper Mill in 1965. Some 20 years after Domtar took over, Thomas Gosling relocated his family to Cornwall, to take that job working for the mill.

In an interview with *Jam! Showbiz*, Ryan said that going into acting as a career meant that he was the first of 12 males in his family to break with tradition in not working for a paper mill. It's not clear whether all of those relatives worked at the Domtar Paper Mill too, or if they all just so happened to be in the same industry, working for different paper mills. Nor is it clear if they were all on his father's side of the family tree or if they were also from his mother's family. In any case, the fact that the sons all followed in the footsteps of their fathers and took work at a paper mill gives us a picture of what kind of family Ryan was born into: one of tradition. In any case, Ryan would break the generational pattern by opting for a different path in life.

Growing up, Ryan was incredibly close to his sister Mandi and often refers to how much he looked up to her when he was a child and how he continues to do so as an adult. As is almost always the case, as the younger sibling, Ryan would have instinctively followed in his sister's footsteps, wanting to do whatever she did.

When he turned four, it was time for Ryan to start kindergarten. Had he been born in the first half of 1980, he might have begun school at the age of five, but having turned four before the end of 1984 – the admissions cut-off for elementary school – he was deemed old enough by the system to be enrolled early. This means he started kindergarten in September 1985, when he was four years and ten months old.

It's difficult to pin down the elementary school attended by Ryan due to the varied accounts of the path of his education. Some reports say that he began his elementary school education at East Front Public School in Cornwall, Ontario. The school still exists today and can be found at 1810 Montreal Road in Cornwall. However, there are other reports that do not mention Ryan attending East Front Public School and instead say that he started his education at Gladstone Public School, which can also be found in Cornwall, at 825 McConnell Avenue. Due to this dual reporting, it's possible that he went to both schools in quick succession, starting at one and then switching to the other, for reasons we can only imagine.

Back home, Ryan was introduced to his lifelong love of music by his mother, a big fan of the Beatles, who often played music by the Fab Four on the family's hi-fi system. Ryan would later tell *The Huffington Post* about how many memories he had of the Beatles sound-tracking his childhood, how hearing certain songs transported him straight back to the past. When asked to reveal his favourite Beatles song, he told the reporter it was 'Here, There and Everywhere', a track that features on their 1966 album *Revolver*. Of all the songs in their catalogue to choose, 'Here, There and Everywhere' is an interesting choice as it is sometimes ranked by Paul McCartney as one of his own personal favourite Beatles songs.

McCartney apparently wrote the song by the swimming pool at John Lennon's house in Weybridge, Surrey. He had arrived one day to find that his bandmate was not yet awake and, while waiting for him, he sat strumming away on his guitar until he suddenly found himself struck by a thunderclap of spontaneous inspiration. By the time Lennon had woken, McCartney had half written the song and debuted it for him. Liking the direction it was taking, they finished it, as was their magic, on the spot.

Though the Beatles were an important force in the Gosling household, nothing held as much sway as their Mormon faith. According to *GQ* magazine, Ryan's parents were converted to the religion by door-to-door Mormon missionaries, who turned up on the doorstep proselytising and found what they had to say went down well.

There is no more detail in the public domain that goes into more depth as to how or why this happened. Were either or both of the Goslings religious in any form before the doorbell rang? Had they been raised within a particular faith, which they then abandoned, in order to follow The Church of Jesus Christ of Latter-day Saints? Regardless of the answers to these questions and, more than that, how their conversion happened – instantly or over a period of visits – the Goslings (and particularly Donna) reportedly took to the Mormon faith with zeal and commitment. As a result, Ryan and Mandi were raised within the Mormon Church.

In interviews, Ryan has often said that his parents were not particularly strict Mormons and that, while the family did take the faith seriously, Donna was always careful to stress that it was just one faith and, if he and Mandi felt differently to their parents, then that was absolutely fine. In short, although this has sometimes been wrongly inferred, Ryan was most definitely not raised in a strict religious home.

The Church of Jesus Christ of Latter-day Saints was founded by Joseph Smith in Fayette, New York State in April 1830, following a vision that came to him in 1820, when God and Jesus both apparently appeared as the 14-year-old Smith prayed to God for guidance as to which church he should become a member of. The same year as the Mormon Church was founded, Smith also orchestrated the publication of 5,000 copies of *The Book of Mormon* in Palmyra, New York.

In terms of what Mormons believe, The Church of Jesus Christ of Latter-day Saints website summarises their belief system as follows: 'We are all spiritual children of a loving Heavenly Father who sent us to this earth to learn and grow in a mortal state. As Mormons, we are followers of Jesus Christ. We live our lives to serve Him and teach of His eternal plan for each of us.'

Mormons use *The Book of Mormon* as well as the Bible for worship. They believe that the site of the Garden of Eden, where God placed Adam and Eve, is located in Jackson County, Missouri.

Their beliefs play a number of roles in their everyday lives, not least that it is a central premise of the faith that sees today's estimated 13 million Mormons living a high level of attachment to family and so-called traditional family values. In terms of lifestyle choices, Mormons must obey a lengthy list of acts and substances that are forbidden, including the drinking of both tea and coffee, the smoking of tobacco, homosexuality, gambling, sex before marriage, abortion and pornography.

One of the aspects at the heart of Mormon life with which Ryan certainly connected was the warm sense of community – he found this coming together with like-minded people to be positive and comforting. He especially liked the services, which gave him an opportunity to sing in church, as he later told *Beliefnet*: 'There's good things about going to church. Being Mormon socialized me at a young age. You have to pray in public, shake a lot of hands, talk in public, sing in church, stuff like that.'

Thomas Gosling was often away travelling for work. This was natural, given that he was a salesman for the print mill and was often out on the road, selling his company's services to prospective new clients and expanded contracts to existing ones. On account of his father being away so much, though, from a young age Ryan grew up very attached to his mother and sister, and he has often said that he became conditioned by their feminine company. He later talked about that feminine influence in an interview with *The Sunday Times*, saying, 'I feel that I think like a girl, just through osmosis, really, living with my mom and my sister. They talk so much. If you live in a house with just women when your brain is forming, well, I think my thought process became more similar to a woman's. I talk to my friends and I feel a connection. A lot of my friends grew up with single mothers. And it's like we communicate differently. I never spent a lot of time around guys.'

If comments Ryan later made to *The Toronto Star* are anything to go by, his early school years were happy ones.

'Canada's a really beautiful country,' he told them. 'And it was nice to grow up in such a multicultural place where racial differences never really entered my mind. I went to kindergarten with people of every colour of the rainbow and my first crush was on an Indian girl.'

As his education began, he started to have intense daydreams. He later told *The Sun* that, in these daydreams, he'd want to place himself in the same realm as cars: 'I also stood in the middle of the street trying to get hit by cars, not because I wanted to die but I wanted to be where the cars were.' This seems to be an early example of how effectively Ryan could transport himself deep into an altered reality and really believe it – something he would come to do so effectively as an actor.

He also got up to a lot of typically boyish mischief, giving his parents a hard time, as he later recalled in an interview with the *Daily Telegraph*: 'From as early as two years old, I was sneaking out of the house, never wearing my clothes, breaking things, putting the cat in the drier and setting the house on fire. I also remember that I kept stealing a girl neighbour out of her house. It was when we were both about two. I'd steal her away and try to take her on dates!'

Taking his mind off such mischief, when Ryan was six, he was introduced to the spectacle of public performance and entertainment via an uncle.

The relative in question was Ryan's uncle Perry, who was a massive Elvis Presley fan. In his spare time, he put on an Elvis impersonator act under the stage name of 'Elvis Perry'. The way Ryan tells it, his uncle bore little resemblance to Elvis

Presley, yet he believed so wholeheartedly that he made a great Elvis impersonator that his performances – at least from where his nephew was standing – were phenomenal: so exciting, so dynamic, that his credentials for putting on a tribute show seemed impossible to challenge.

Ryan has spoken of tagging along with Uncle Perry as he put on his show in venues such as shopping malls. Watching from the wings, with a child's large eyes, as his uncle gyrated and belted out his Elvis songs, he saw how he would drive his audiences to wild, enthusiastic applause. MSN Movies quoted his recalling how he felt about joining his uncle's performances: 'Suddenly I'm in the act – I'm head of security and I have this jacket, and I'm walking out and I can hear all these screaming people and suddenly my uncle, who has a moustache, a birthmark and no hair and looks nothing like Elvis, he became Elvis. He gets on stage and he's amazing.'

Ryan was also fascinated by the way his uncle assumed this theatrical persona, and would linger transfixed before the shows as Perry changed into his stage costume – more often than not, a jumpsuit – and worked his hair into a perfect, reverent Elvis quiff. Those foundation basics prepared, Ryan would then watch his uncle add decorative jewellery. This process of assembling a character for performance would prove supremely influential later on when Ryan would develop a character for a part he was playing, as he recalled to MSN Movies, 'I was six so I didn't really know what I wanted but I'm sure that that had to have something to do with it. He taught me how to build a character.'

When you think of Ryan agonising over choosing the

perfect brand of toothpick for the Driver to chew on in *Drive* or gaining enough weight to portray an inert character like Lars in *Lars And The Real Girl*, it's hard not to trace the detail involved in that character development work back to those childhood outings where he'd watch his uncle transform himself, detail by detail, into not only an Elvis Presley impersonator, but also a confident showman.

At his uncle's shows, as per a family joke, Ryan was known to serve as head of security. Of course, what he was really doing was tagging along and wherever possible assisting Perry in that desperately keen-to-be-involved-in-every-way manner unique to children. At the same time, like all young boys, Ryan looked up to his uncle and, in a theatrical sense, hero-worshipped the older relative. Ryan later said in an interview that his uncle used to perform a version of Elvis' 1957 hit single 'Teddy Bear' and that his job was to theatrically hand him a teddy bear at a designated point in the song. He no doubt enjoyed that split second of being directly in the spotlight.

At home, like most children, Ryan and his sister loved to listen to bedtime stories. Ryan's absolute favourite was for his mother to read a children's book called *The Giving Tree* to him and Mandi. The book, by Chicago-born author/poet/cartoonist/songwriter/playwright Shel Silverstein, was first published in 1964 and tells the heart-wrenching, melancholy tale of the lifelong relationship between a small boy as he grows up and goes through life and a tree that grows and becomes old in tandem with the boy.

Much later, as character preparation, while making the film

Blue Valentine, Ryan would have an illustration from *The Giving Tree* tattooed onto his upper left arm. The image is taken from the jacket cover to the book, where the little boy is standing beneath the tree, waiting to catch an apple falling from a branch. Ryan told *Vulture* what the book means to him: 'That book is so fucked up; that story's the worst. I mean, at the end the tree is a stump and the old guy just sitting on him; he's just used him to death, and you're supposed to want to be the tree? Fuck you. You be the tree. I don't want to be the tree.'

After having enjoyed kindergarten so much, Ryan's relationship with school changed and he began to experience difficulties with the other children, and with his studies. He stood out as a prime target for bullying and other children singled him out for a hard time.

He said later that school would have worked better for him if the pupils had been allowed to get up and walk up and down at the back of a classroom during lessons so they could burn off excess energy whenever they felt that they were losing the ability to properly concentrate on whatever the teacher was trying to tell them.

Faced with this dual academic and social isolation at school, Ryan did what most children experiencing such problems do: he retreated into himself and turned to TV shows and films as a portal to escape into. Later, he spoke of this suddenly difficult period in an interview with *Company* magazine, telling them: 'I was a lonely child, I didn't do well at school and TV was my only friend.'

He has said that he wasn't particularly bothered about not

having any close friends because he didn't really want any – as a child, he was a contented loner, who regarded his mother and sister as his best friends.

One day, he was watching *The Muppet Show* on TV and the special guest star was the voluptuous actress Raquel Welch. The show was a re-run of Episode 11 from Season 3, which had originally aired in 1978.

In one scene in the show, Welch was involved in a song which required her – in typical, brilliant kids-pleasing *Muppet Show* fashion – to dance with a large, furry spider. In a prehistoric setting – obviously designed to reference her performance in the epic 1966 film *One Million Years B.C.* – she dances enthusiastically to Diana Ross' disco-flavoured track 'Baby It's Me' in high heels and a very skimpy dress, while the gigantic spider kookily sets about doing his best to mimic her every move.

Ryan told *Company* that he found this scene mesmerising, that it completely captured his imagination: 'I immediately fell in love. She was the first crush I ever had and I thought, how do I get to meet this woman? And then I thought, well, she's on TV, so to meet her I have to get on TV myself.'

Aside from being a very cute story, this was rather like Ryan's anecdote about standing out in the street because he wanted to be where the cars were – only in this case, he had beamed himself into a scene in a children's TV show and connected with an actress.

By this point, we can see a picture starting to grow of a young boy who loved the social, community aspects of being a Mormon (in particular, the communal singing and social get-togethers at church), but not the actual religion; a boy who was happy in the multicultural realm of his kindergarten and whose 'first crush' was on an Indian girl; a boy whose favourite children's book was the philosophical tearjerker *The Giving Tree*; a boy who was incredibly close to his mother and sister; a boy who had trouble concentrating at school; a boy whose sensitivity and difference waved like a red rag to bullies at school; a boy who shared his mother's love for the Beatles; a boy who did typical young boy things such as accidentally letting the handbrake off while mesmerised by the mechanics of his parents' car; and, later, the kind of boy who dealt with feeling stressed out by life in school by escaping into TV and developing a crush on Raquel Welch as she danced in a satirically raunchy style with a large, furry spider in an episode of *The Muppet Show*.

Growing up as this cute, sensitive, internalised, alienated boy was setting Ryan up perfectly to play many of the alienated, internalised roles with which he would end up making his name.

CHAPTER TWO

EARLY INFLUENCES

As well as helping out Uncle Perry with his Elvis act, Ryan was keen to pitch in and help his father too, whenever the opportunity presented itself. For instance, Thomas once had a large stock of cellophane and needed to figure out a way to sell it. Even back then, ever keen to work hard, Ryan was struck by an entrepreneurial flash and humped rolls of cellophane neatly aligned in his backpack into school with him, where he attempted to sell rolls to his classmates and other students – all to no avail.

If selling cellophane didn't seem to be his calling in life, he soon found himself stepping closer in the right direction, though.

When he was eight, Ryan reportedly began singing from time to time at weddings. He hasn't said how this happened so we don't know if the gigs came about via Uncle Perry's act or if they were simply weddings that took place at the Goslings' local Mormon church in Cornwall. He told *Interview* magazine what the work typically involved: 'While the bride was sitting on the chair, I would get down on my knees and sing the song, and then my sister would sing another song, and then together we would sing [Bob Seger's hit] "Old Time Rock & Roll". Then sometimes if we were really killing it, I'd sing [Dion's hit] "Runaround Sue."'

Ryan hasn't said if these weddings took place at The Church of Jesus Christ of Latter-day Saints in Cornwall, but, regardless of how these performances came about, they gave Ryan a taste of being in the spotlight and receiving applause for his singing and dancing. That validation, especially for a young boy who was struggling academically and socially at school, must have spoken to him considerably and felt good.

Back home, TV shows and films continued to entrance Ryan, who had now taken a serious liking to old black and white Abbott and Costello movies. The American comic duo Bud Abbott and Lou Costello built a name for themselves as comedians in burlesque shows and then at comedy clubs before moving first into radio, then film – making over 35 classic comedies between 1940 and 1956 – and finally TV, where they sustained continually impressive ratings for *The Abbott and Costello Show*. It would seem likely that Ryan's father introduced his son to Abbott and Costello since they came from a previous generation.

Of their large body of work, Ryan's favourite film was the duo's 1941 classic *Hold That Ghost*. It's a crime caper built around Abbott and Costello's characters who by way of becoming accidentally involved with a gangster end up becoming the owners of what appears to be a haunted tavern. The classic haunted house plot stays faithful to variations on the good old-fashioned ghost story theme that has run throughout Ryan's life, whether expressed through his love of the Haunted Mansion ride at Disneyland and Disney World, or via the spooky band he would later form: Dead Man's Bones.

Ryan's fascination with the supernatural started young. He later told *Esquire* magazine that, in one of his childhood homes, he used to see an old man from time to time, who he believed was a ghost: 'He just sat. And I knew from a very young age that he was a ghost, too. He scared me. I told my mother, but she couldn't see him. Nobody could. And I learned to live with that. I had to. Then, a few years later, she thought she saw him, then almost right away my cousin saw him, and then my uncle. And we were outta there in fairly short order.'

As a child, Ryan also became intrigued by cemeteries and loved using them as a playground. This came about via his mother who was herself fascinated by cemeteries and liked to walk through them, pausing here and there to read the epitaphs on the headstones.

Adding to these spooky anecdotes, nine-year-old Ryan saw the 1989 film *Little Monsters*, starring child star actor Fred Savage as a lonely little boy – Brian Stevenson – who makes friends with Maurice, a monster who lives under his bed. Everybody in his life misunderstands Brian, except for Maurice.

Ryan was also developing a taste for action movies. He

especially liked the 1985 film *Commando*, which starred Arnold Schwarzenegger, Rae Dawn Chong and Alyssa Milano. Another action movie that had a big impact on him was *First Blood* (1982), starring Sylvester Stallone as John Rambo, a misunderstood and unjustly hounded Vietnam veteran, on the run from a small-town police department who misread him as a trouble-making drifter.

Rambo's story provoked an intense connection in Ryan, so much so that, when the film ended, he felt as if he was John Rambo and the movie was simply playing on. He told *About.com* that the connection was completely absorbing: 'When I first saw *First Blood* it put a spell on me and I thought I was Rambo. I even thought my face felt like Sylvester Stallone's face when I touched it.'

But the story didn't stop with Ryan feeling as if his face was that of Sylvester Stallone – it continued all the way into the next day. He headed into school with a set of steak knives packed inside his Fisher Price Houdini magic kit. During break, he took out the knives and enacted what would appear to be interpretations of scenes from the movie. 'I took them and threw them at all the kids during recess,' he told *About.com*. 'I got suspended, rightfully so.'

This episode demonstrates how Ryan could watch a film and stay in character afterwards and how easily he was able to do that – he would of course later become known in his work as an actor for seamlessly entering characters and penetrating roles so entirely that it was as if he became those characters.

Ryan's parents were understandably horrified by the incident as Ryan recalled in an interview with the *Daily*

Telegraph: 'It wasn't until I got suspended and my mother slapped me out of it that I realised I wasn't in that movie any more. I wasn't allowed to watch R-rated movies after that. I would only watch Abbott and Costello, and National Geographic films.'

This also meant Ryan's parents steering him towards movies with a biblical theme – for instance Cecil B. DeMille's 1956 epic *The Ten Commandments*, starring Charlton Heston.

Ryan has stated quite clearly that none of the problems he was experiencing with fitting in at school had anything to do with what was going on at home; instead, it was all down to his finding it hard to be a child and wanting to be grown up already, a point he underlined when talking with the *Daily Telegraph* in 2008: 'None of my behaviour was prompted by my home life. It was more that I just wanted to be a man, have a job, a real place, date girls and get on with it.'

Asked by the newspaper why he behaved in this way and what motivated such episodes, Ryan said that he felt like his life at school was overly structured and made him feel as if he had no say in what his days were filled with or how he spent them. He revealed that he didn't handle childhood at all well: 'Being a kid made me crazy; I was doing crazy things because I felt very claustrophobic and panicky.'

This feeling came to a head when the school told Thomas and Donna that they were contemplating moving Ryan into a special needs class, where, on account of his problems concentrating, he'd receive more focused attention from his teachers. The school must have thought that this would be the best way to support his development. The Goslings were not remotely interested, though, in having their son shunted into a special needs class, so the decision was made that Ryan would instead be taken out of school altogether and Donna would leave her job as a secretary in order to home school her son.

She felt he needed that one-to-one attention; also that he must be liberated from a way of learning that did not suit him and he had to get out of an environment where he was being bullied. After all, nothing kills a child's desire to learn faster than being in an unsafe environment.

The decision seems to have been the right one. Ryan was relieved to be plucked from the turmoil of school and to take a year out in the safety and comfort of the family home. Under Donna's tutelage, he spent his days in the company of an excellent teacher who understood him, and of course loved him dearly. Ryan credits her with rebuilding his self-esteem, using teaching strategies that worked around the difficulties he had in concentrating. He sang her praises in an interview with *About.com* while promoting *The Notebook*, saying, 'When I was in school, she took me out of school for a year to teach me. She homeschooled me. I think that that meant a lot to me and she showed me a lot of support. I was like in the fifth grade or something, but wasn't really cutting it. So she kind of took the time to do that.'

Instead of berating him for being restless, as the school had, Donna taught around it. If he started to find it hard to concentrate, she let him run off some energy before they went back to whatever they were studying. Working at his pace, she would employ strategies such as unrolling one of the large rolls of paper the family had stored in their basement and encouraging him to draw pictures on the paper around the theme of their latest topic. In this way, she was able to restore and redirect his natural curiosity back to learning.

Ryan has also said that during that year at home, when he was 10 and 11, his mother introduced him to the jazz music of Chet Baker and Billie Holiday and he was allowed to watch a lot of films. He liked Baker and Holiday and their cool attitude, and being introduced to artists such as this struck him as a different, but no less important form of attending school, too.

Meanwhile, Ryan increasingly looked up to his older sister and wanted to emulate her. He told the *Independent* that he spent so much time with his mother and sister growing up that it taught him a feminine sensibility: 'I think like a girl. I was literally raised by my mother and my sister. And I feel like I wouldn't know how to think any other way.'

This played out in lots of ways. For instance, Ryan would watch his sister studying ballet and think it looked amazing and want to learn it, too. It's a common scenario with brothers and sisters. Even though, in a *Billy Elliot* way, most boys during this era who expressed an interest in studying ballet to their parents would have been discouraged, Ryan's mother was open to anything he wanted to explore and that got him excited. She promptly signed him up for ballet classes too. As he told the *Independent*, 'I did ballet, which was always just girls. All that stuff had an effect on my brain.'

These stories are very important and explain Ryan's closeness to his mother. She allowed him the freedom to be himself, especially during a time when being himself at school had caused him to be pushed around and beaten up, or landed him in trouble with his teachers. During that year, he was given the breathing room to be himself and his mother's gift to him set him on track for the future.

Another thing that happened during the home-schooling year was that Ryan, like most 11-year-olds, started to show an interest in pop music. He went through a phase of idolising Michael Jackson and then another of idolising Billy Idol.

The Michael Jackson phase undoubtedly inspired him to want to sing and dance and move with the same lightning moves as his idol. It's also no great stretch of the imagination to picture him loving the spookily themed 'Thriller' video, with its Hammer Horror, mock blood-curdling Vincent Price voiceover.

Between ballet lessons and Michael Jackson's music, Ryan, no doubt inspired by his sister's love of singing and dancing, began to think that what he wanted was to work towards becoming a professional dancer. As he began studying and practising, this new focus found an outlet in occasional, ongoing public performances with Mandi.

In summer 2012, a three-and-a-half-minute-long clip of the Gosling siblings performing at what was described as a talent show at The Church of Jesus Christ of Latter-day Saints in Cornwall, filmed by a member of the audience, turned up on YouTube. It quickly went viral, attracting in excess of 100,000 views in the first 24 hours after being posted.

The clip shows Ryan and Mandi wearing matching outfits – red and blue satin shirts and baggy, black MC Hammer-style harem-style trousers – belting out an animated version of his wedding-singer staple 'When A Man Loves A Woman'. He looks like he's having a lot of fun and loves being an entertainer. More than that, he shows off a phenomenal energy and surprising aptitude as a dancer – no wonder he was seriously contemplating a career as a professional dancer around this time – and, in the second half, he and his sister can be seen dancing furiously to C&C Music Factory's 1990 single 'Gonna Make You Sweat (Everybody Dance Now)'.

The clip is interesting in so far as it gives us a portal into how serious Ryan actually was about performing. When he says that standing on the flanks of his uncle Perry's Elvis impersonator act inspired him to want to become an entertainer and a performer himself, and then when one sees this talent-show clip, it's apparent that his desire to appear on stage had now become manifest.

Singing and dancing aside, when the end of the academic year came around, Ryan, now 11, and his mother decided it was time for her to go back to work and him to school.

For Ryan, the home-schooling year had achieved many great things, not least giving him space to be himself and to find out more about what he liked and what he wanted to do. His horizons had been opened up and now he was dreaming on a large scale. He didn't see himself grinding through the rest of his school days and then starting work at a paper mill, unlike his male relatives. Instead, he wanted to find a shortcut and circumnavigate or jump altogether the path laid before him.

Later, he attempted to explain this impatience to grow up and be 'there' already in an interview with the *Guardian*: 'I didn't want to work in a paper mill, and I wasn't going to stay in school. I hated being a kid. I didn't like being told what to do, I didn't like my body – I didn't like any of it. Being a kid and playing and all that stuff just drove me nuts.'

With feelings as strong as this, it was clear that Ryan would all too soon be looking to his singing and dancing skills to buy him an escape ticket from the route set before him and to open a door onto the life he truly desired.

'MOUSE BOY'

G oing back to school meant starting high school. Ryan was enrolled at Cornwall Collegiate and Vocational School, which was founded in 1806. It's one of the oldest schools in Canada and can be found at 437 Sydney Street in Cornwall, where today it has approximately 850 students enrolled.

While he was no doubt nervous about re-entering the formal education system, given that things had become bad enough at his old school that his parents had no choice but to withdraw him from the education system and home school him, the truth was that Ryan had undergone substantial changes during his year at home, thanks to his mother's amazing, intuitive tutelage. As a result, he settled into his new school quickly and easily.

On account of his passion and talent for singing and dancing, he gravitated towards drama classes, where he shone.

His singing ability also marked him out for recognition and praise from the teachers, who advocated for him to become a key member of the school choir. Despite finding a way to build on his interest in singing and dancing within the framework of school life – a framework that had at times felt like a cage to him – Ryan wanted to break out of the school path ahead of him and, in 1993, barely a year after he started his high school education, a once-in-a-lifetime opportunity popped up, offering that escape route.

There are two accounts of how Ryan came to this life-changing opportunity. In the first account, which is the one most often cited, the story begins with his sister Mandi spotting an item in a newspaper about an audition that was to be held in Montreal. The audition was taking place in a bid to search for potential new Mouseketeers to join a revival of the hugely popular Disney TV show *The All New Mickey Mouse Club*.

Mandi scanned the audition announcement, checking the small print, since she herself was thinking of trying out, but then noticed that she was too old for the specified age group and was disappointed. She showed it to Ryan and suggested that he should go and perform in the audition since he was in the specified age bracket. An excited Ryan ended up going along to try out.

In the other account of how Ryan came to attend those auditions, which appears in only one or two sources, he has said that, once he learned that many of the girls in his dance class were to audition for *The All New Mickey Mouse Club* TV show, he figured that, if they were going to try out and he was in the same class as them and, therefore, at the same level, then there was no logic to his not going along to the auditions and giving it his best shot, too.

Regardless of which path led him there, he turned up and quickly discovered that Disney were taking the process very seriously. The auditions lasted for a total of three full days, during which time each hopeful had to demonstrate and prove they could sing, act and dance and, of course, blow the Disney panel away with exceptional talent and an evident charisma.

At one point during the auditions, everybody trying out was given a script to learn and two songs to master. While many trembled under the pressure, Ryan took it all in his stride. What's more, he was having a great time and enjoying the warm hospitality that Disney were extending towards himself and his family. After the number of hopefuls had thinned and thinned until only a cluster of contenders remained, he couldn't believe his luck when the auditions finally came to an end and he was told that he had been chosen to become one of the new Mouseketeers. It was then that he found out that he had beaten 15,000 – some reports increase that figure to 17,000 – other talented children to rise to the top and become another of Canada's very rare Mouseketeers.

On account of his being the first Canadian to join the show, Ryan was invited on the television show *CTV Canada AM* to talk about how he was chosen and what this lucky break meant to him. 'I hit the roof it was so fun,' he said, as he sat there on TV in a denim shirt and patterned tie, looking very much like a clean-cut and confident Macaulay Culkin lookalike. He also explained some of the practicalities, namely that he had been signed up as one of seven new Mouseketeers for the show and that he wouldn't be expected to wear any costume – just his own clothes. Ryan was also asked how his friends had responded to his big break and he simply smiled and said they had taken to calling him 'Mouse Boy'.

The interview ended with his being asked if there was anybody he hoped to meet on the show and he grinned and said that he would love to have the opportunity to meet Michael Jackson, making it clear that he was still in awe of his icon.

Of course, accepting the role on the show meant leaving a school that was still relatively new to him, but Ryan was fine about that – he was ecstatic, in fact, to have managed to head off the prospect of spending his entire adolescence as a slave to the high school schedule. Naturally, he had to stay on track academically and Disney would offer all their Mouseketeers the services of private tutors, so they could carry on with the same curriculum that they would have been studying, had they been attending their regular high schools.

Ryan's contract saw him hired for Seasons 6 and 7 of the series. The first season was to start shooting in May 1993. This popular children's variety show, revived in 1989 after a near 20-year sabbatical, had first launched as *The Mickey Mouse Club* in 1955 and enjoyed a successful run all the way until 1960. After a lengthy break, it returned in a modernised format to air again between 1977 and 1979. Noticing the re-runs were attracting decent viewing figures, Disney decided to dust down the show and re-launch it in 1989 as *The All New Mickey Mouse Club*. It was for this incarnation that Ryan was hired.

When they arrived in Florida, Ryan and his family discovered that most of the Mouseketeers and their families lived in Kissimmee, in an apartment building. They explored this as an option but the rent was beyond their reach so they set about finding alternative accommodation as quickly as possible. They ended up settling into a new home in Kissimmee – but in a nearby trailer park in Yogi Bear's Jellystone Park.

Once he began work on the show, Ryan found himself in the company of some exceptionally gifted young entertainers. In this beehive of talent, he worked alongside a spectacular roll call of future stars including Britney Spears, Christina Aguilera and Justin Timberlake. Ryan later told *The Sunday Times* that he and Britney Spears became friends: 'Britney was a sweetheart. She lived right above me, the girl next door. The little girl I used to play basketball and spin the bottle with.'

Once filming started in May, Ryan was surprised to find that work on the show was far less intensive than he was expecting and often he found himself with time on his hands. To fill his time, he would make the most of the free passes given to him by Disney and entire afternoons would be lost daydreaming in the Disney World park.

He would wander about and enjoy seeing performers on breaks backstage – for instance, a man enjoying a cup of coffee in full costume with a head mask tucked under his arm – and he'd also take the rides. On the topic of rides, Ryan developed a major fascination with the Haunted Mansion, which he would go on as often as he could.

That one ride in particular would go on to wield its

influence on him permanently, so much so that he continues to enjoy it to this day and, when he was putting his band, Dead Man's Bones, together, the ride proved to be a bonding agent of sorts, since all three people connected to the band – Ryan, Zach Shields and Tim Anderson – discovered that the others also held a reverence for the Haunted Mansion ride and the classic Disney albums *Chilling, Thrilling Sounds of The Haunted House* (1964) and *The Story and Song from the Haunted Mansion* (1969) which featured stories accompanied by sound effects, released in its honour by Disney.

Ryan used those days wandering about Disney World as a chance to process what was happening to him. He had, after all, been given a tremendous break and now here he was living in Florida, far away from Cornwall, Ontario and from the life that he should have been experiencing back at his old high school, where the zenith of his week would have been singing in the choir. There was a lot for him to get his head around, a lot of adjusting to do. Overnight, he was living in a fantasy world.

Spending the next 18 months wandering about Disney World in his free time and riding the Haunted Mansion ride, over and over, meant, as he later told *Esquire* magazine, that he effectively 'went through puberty in a theme park'. As puberty came on and he lived in this bubble, he saw this phase as a magical time, a prolonged fantasy, in which he was plucked out of reality and dropped into a landscape where everything existed in a world of make believe.

Ever since this time, Ryan has visited Disneyland in Anaheim, California – the park nearest to him since he established a home in Los Angeles at the age of 17. It's as if that park is a sacred place for him. He goes to Disneyland to reconnect with the energy and the magic he first discovered in Disney World between the ages of 12 and 13. That special time can be tapped into whenever he visits either Disney park; today, he says he goes to Disneyland three or four times a year and sometimes he goes alone to take the rides, listening to Brian Eno albums on his headphones. Other times, he goes in the company of close friends or girlfriends or family. Though his favourite ride is still the Haunted Mansion, he says that the Enchanted Tiki Room follows right behind as a close second. Later on, he would even celebrate a milestone birthday at Disneyland.

Despite beating 15,000 hopefuls to secure his role, Ryan still felt nervous surrounded by such a high pedigree of talent. Often he would watch Christina Aguilera singing and dancing and be struck by how much she loved this work and that it was clearly her destiny. This told him that he didn't feel the same way. He later reflected on his doubts in conversation with *Interview* magazine, saying, 'It was kind of depressing because, when I got there, they realized that I wasn't really up to snuff in comparison with what some of the other kids were able to do.'

When he was on set working, rehearsing for an episode or filming the actual Disney show, he became increasingly good friends with fellow Mouseketeer Justin Timberlake, who clearly didn't share Ryan's misgivings. Later, Timberlake would tell *Playboy* that he noticed Ryan's talent from the offset, saying, 'I thought he had charisma that was just beaming, which has turned out to serve him really well as an actor.'

For Ryan, the best times were spent messing about with his friend Justin Timberlake, or when he could roam alone throughout the Disney park on a free pass, as he told *Entertainment Weekly*: 'I walked around eating those big turkey legs and riding Space Mountain and puking my brains out. It was awesome.'

When Season 6 premiered on TV on 4 October 1993, in the opening credits, each of the 20 Mouseketeers called out his or her name. When Ryan appeared, calling out 'Ryan!', he looked very young, dressed in the class Mouseketeer baseball jacket, with his name emblazoned over the breast in capital letters. The new season, featuring Ryan, would air until 2 December 1993 and feature 35 episodes.

Around this time, things were apparently turbulent at home. Various respected newspapers have reported that Ryan's parents separated soon after the family decamped to Florida. But quite a few other sources contradict this, appearing to suggest that Thomas and Donna instead separated some time before this, when Ryan was much younger.

The *Daily Telegraph* reports the separation as happening in Florida: '[It was in Florida] where his parents' marriage finally hit the rocks and he found himself the family's wage-earner.' The *Observer* appears to concur with this: 'While his parents divorced, he lived at Justin Timberlake's house for a while.'

Ryan has never passed any public comment on his parents' separation and divorce, so we have no insights into how he feels about what happened, and there is no information in the public domain to explain why the marriage broke down or how it affected Ryan or his sister.

However, in a 2013 *Sunday Times Style* magazine feature on Ryan, it was reported that, when Ryan got his break and moved to Florida, he headed down there with his mother and sister – while his father remained in Canada. The article appears to allege that, during this time of living apart, the marriage broke down.

With regard to Ryan going to live with Justin Timberlake and his family, it has also never been made clear why, but, in the middle of work on Season 7 of the show, it would seem Donna Gosling needed to go back to Canada for work reasons. Therefore, she had to arrange for a legal guardian to take over custody of Ryan so that he could continue with his work on *The All New Mickey Mouse Club* and she could return to Ontario with Ryan's sister, Mandi. The solution was for Ryan to briefly move in with Justin Timberlake's family and Timberlake's mother, Lynn, became his legal guardian for a temporary period of six months.

During this time, Ryan and Justin had a lot of fun together, whether hanging out and eating ice cream, enjoying the Disney World rides together or goofing about as 13-year-old boys tend to do, as Timberlake recalled in an interview on *The Jonathan Ross Show*: 'We were partners in crime for a short amount of time... Aw, man, we were crazy. We, like, skipped tutoring. Going to the park, to the *Honey I Shrunk The Kids* set. We'd have milkshakes. Oh, man, we were so gangster.'

Towards the end of work on Season 7, Ryan found out that Disney were closing down the show and that this season was to be the last. This meant that Ryan and all the other Mouseketeers would be out of work come the end of October

1994, when Disney would wrap the filming. At that time, Ryan packed up and left Justin Timberlake's home and returned to Canada to live with his mother and sister. It was time to say goodbye to the Disney fantasy he'd been living in and go back to high school.

CHAPTER FOUR

FIRST BREAKS
AND BRANDO

When Ryan returned to Canada, it would appear that he likely moved briefly back to Cornwall, Ontario, resuming his studies at the Cornwall Collegiate and Vocational school. At high school, he was less vulnerable than before, but still different – now, of course, he was singled out for having been a child star and Mouseketeer on TV. And, having had that experience for two years, it would have been a crash back to earth to suddenly be clocking in for school again.

As he settled back into high school life, Ryan was to undergo the kind of personal development typical of a 14-year-old. He had come to the conclusion that the Mormon faith wasn't for him and told his mother he felt this way. As ever, she respected his choice and his decision, encouraging him to go his own way spiritually.

Moving on from his earlier love of action movies and Michael Jackson, he was also in the process of discovering and seeking out a whole new spread of music and films that spoke to him more precisely about where he was at in his life and what kind of person he was. One such discovery came about via the family's local video shop. Ryan was a dedicated regular, always stopping by to rent movies, and, one day, an employee at the store recommended that he rent David Lynch's sinister, disturbing 1986 film *Blue Velvet*.

Taking up the recommendation, Ryan took the movie home and was mesmerised by Lynch's vision as a screenwriter and fearless directing, as well as by the strong performances from Isabella Rossellini and Kyle MacLachlan, topped off by Dennis Hopper's completely out there, demented and unforgettable Frank Booth. Seeing this film caused something of an epiphany for Ryan: after watching it, he knew that, in future, he wanted to play a part in producing work that could be similarly powerful and uncompromising that it would move audiences with its unflinching intensity.

The other discovery Ryan made at this time was the music of gravel-voiced singer/songwriter Tom Waits, whose poetic tales of American realism set to music variously jazzy, blues, avant garde and rock 'n' roll also struck a chord. He liked Waits' way with words and his romantic celebrations of the bohemian lifestyle that beat writers such as Jack Kerouac, Allen Ginsberg and William S. Burroughs and jazz musicians such as Chet Baker, Charlie Parker, Miles Davis and John Coltrane all pioneered and personified before him.

Waits' story also shone a spotlight on integrity within

Hollywood, since the musician had long been involved with highly regarded projects, including scoring Francis Ford Coppola's *One From The Heart* (in which Waits also made a fleeting cameo) and acting in acclaimed films, also by Coppola, such as *The Outsiders*, *Rumble Fish*, *The Cotton Club*, *Dracula*, *Short Cuts*, *Down By Law* and *Mystery Train*.

Both discoveries are highly regarded artists and what this meant was that Ryan was gravitating to their seriousness as artists and assimilating their values, their integrity, their credibility. Such an aligning meant that he saw his own future as being very different to that of the Mouseketeers he had worked alongside. He was starting to project a far more serious future for himself, one in which he too would be highly regarded.

Back in his present reality, though, Season 7 of *The All New Mickey Mouse Club* premiered on TV on 4 May 1995. In the new opening credits, the Mouseketeers appeared onscreen one by one, only this time, instead of just their first names, their full names flashed onscreen. As Ryan's name appears on the screen, he is shown in a stripy T-shirt, talking on the phone and smiling. With his abundant onscreen charisma, you can see how much he has grown up between the premieres of Seasons 6 and 7.

Around this time, when Ryan was in his early to mid-teens, it appears that he and his family relocated to Burlington, Ontario. At this time, in late 1994, Burlington had a population of just over 136,000 people. The city, which sits at the southwestern end of Lake Ontario, is a short drive from Hamilton and a 31-mile drive from Toronto. Like Cornwall, it started out as a settlement and was then given the name of Burlington when it was designated a village in 1872. As a reflection of its steady growth, it was given the status of a town some 40 years later, in 1915.

In this new city, Ryan was enrolled at the Lester B. Pearson High School, which can be found at 1433 Headon Road in Burlington. Even after settling in, Ryan found days spent in classrooms confining after a life employed by Disney, which had involved rehearsing, filming and many an afternoon when he was free to roam about Disney World in a daydream, enjoying the rides and a sense of space.

With *The All New Mickey Mouse Club* show back on TV again, Ryan was able to use his Disney profile as a calling card and have his mother take him to auditions. Very quickly he won his first acting break – which is always the way for Ryan: whatever he turns his ambition towards happens fast. The part was a guest role in a TV series called *Are You Afraid Of The Dark?* The American/Canadian co-produced children's show, which delivered a weekly paranormal-themed episode centred on a core nucleus of teenagers who comprise 'the Midnight Society', aired on TV from 1990 until 1996.

Ryan appeared in an episode titled 'The Tale of Station 109.1', playing a character called Jamie Leary. This particular episode aired on Canadian TV on 4 November 1995, a week before he celebrated his 15th birthday. The show often featured guest actors and it also proved to be a fertile place to win a credit for fellow Ontario native, actress Neve Campbell, who soon afterwards found success with her role in the long-standing TV show *Party of Five*.

Now that Ryan had that crucial first acting foot in the door, he was able to land another guest role in the Canadian teen drama series *Ready Or Not?*. This show, which enjoyed a healthy run from 1993 to 1997, followed the ongoing tale of a friendship between two teenage girls, Amanda Zimm (played by Laura Bertram) and Elizabeth 'Busy' Ramone (Lani Billard). Created by Alyse Rosenberg, the series was filmed on location in Canada. Ryan made a guest appearance as Matt Kalinsky in Season 4, for the fifth episode, titled 'I Do, I Don't'.

This particular episode, which aired on TV in 1996, revolves around a storyline about 'Busy' Ramone and her brother. Ryan appears with Kurt Cobain-style blond hair. In one scene, he wears a sheepskin coat and, in another, a super baggy grey sweater. He looks a little like Michael Pitt, whom Ryan would later act alongside in *Murder By Numbers* (2002).

The more TV parts he was able to add to his résumé, the more parts he was able to audition for, and the rest of 1995 passed with Ryan juggling school, while racking up a swift run of further TV appearances – all guest roles. His school was supportive of his blossoming success and happy to excuse him every time he needed to film.

In his spare time, he continued to devour films and, after seeing *East Of Eden*, the 1955 Elia Kazan classic, he quickly added it to his list of all-time favourites. One can see James Dean's performance in that movie, as well as in *Rebel Without A Cause* and *Giant*, as having a significant influence on Ryan's acting later on: in particular Dean's way of mumbling when speaking, his multitude of facial expressions and the use of his body to denote a character's feelings.

At the same time, Ryan also feasted on films featuring Marlon Brando, such as *The Godfather*, *Superman*, *On The Waterfront*, *The Wild One*, *A Streetcar Named Desire*, *Last Tango In Paris* and *Apocalypse Now*, and began to study Brando's trademark mumble of an accent, before working on imitating it to the best of his ability. In time, he successfully transformed his own soft Canadian timbre into the studied, talking-to-myself-while-busy-chewing-gum mumble with which Brando mesmerised audiences, over and over.

On assuming this new Brando-inspired accent, Ryan would later tell *W* magazine: 'As a kid I decided that a Canadian accent doesn't sound tough. I thought guys should sound like Marlon Brando. So now I have a phony accent that I can't shake, so it's not phony anymore.'

When he wasn't stockpiling influences, he was pushing ahead with his acting work. The first of several parts to come in quick succession was a role in *Goosebumps*, a popular Canadian TV show, based on the children's horror books of the same name by R.L. Stine. Ryan turned up in an episode called 'Say Cheese And Die', playing the part of Greg Banks. His appearance came in Episode 15 of Season 1 and he co-starred with Renessa Blitz, Akiva Salzman, Caley Wilson and Richard McMillan. The episode aired on TV on 9 February 1996. It was Ryan's first high-profile part – he had top billing and he was almost constantly onscreen throughout.

Road To Avonlea, another Canadian/US-produced TV series, based on a classic series of books by L.M. Montgomery, gave him his next part. This long-standing show, which ran from 1990 to 1996, saw Ryan cast as Bret McNulty in an episode titled 'From Away', which first aired on TV on 3 March 1996.

Ryan plays one of two British orphans who have been lured to the Avonlea home on the pretence that they are going to be adopted, only to find that they are instead put to work. In the episode, Ryan has to put on an English accent, which doesn't come off at all well, to the point where he ends up sounding as if he's speaking with a peculiar mash-up of Cockney, Australian and South African accents.

Next up was a part in *Kung Fu: The Legend Continues*, the latest incarnation of the ever-popular TV show *Kung Fu*, which starred David Carradine. Ryan was given the role of Kevin in Season 4, Episode 9, which was called 'Dragon's Lair'. The episode screened on 13 May 1996.

Then came a guest role that lasted for two episodes of the same show – a sure sign that Ryan was slowly pushing his way deeper into the world of TV. *Flash Forward*, a Canadian-produced Disney Channel series, lasted for a single 21-episode season over 1996/97. The show revolved around two lifelong friends and neighbours, Tucker and Becca, played by Ben Foster and Jewel Staite, forced to deal with the various challenges associated with being students in the eighth grade at school.

Ryan appeared twice as a character by the name of Scott Stuckey, first in Episode 11 ('Double Bill') and then again, ten weeks later, in Episode 21 ('Skate Bait'). In the first episode, his character was involved in a double-date scenario with

Becca and her friend Christine and then, in the second, Scott was meant to take part in an ice-skating face-off with a character called Gooch. Instead, Gooch bails out and passes the challenge to Tucker.

The flurry of TV roles that year came to a conclusion with a guest role in the Canadian sci-fi series *PSI Factor: Chronicles of the Paranormal*, which was hosted by *Ghostbusters* star Dan Aykroyd. Ryan played Adam in the opening episode of Season 1, titled 'Dream House/UFO Encounter', which premiered on Canadian TV on 28 September 1996.

Even as Ryan's TV work stacked up and his reputation grew, his parallel interest in more serious acting – as personified by the careers of Marlon Brando and James Dean – would increasingly fire up in him a desire to move away from TV. For now, though, his goal was to land a recurring role on a TV show, which would offer continuity and an end to constant dipping in and out of different shows.

CHAPTER FIVE

FIRST STEPS
IN FILM

Just shy of his 16th birthday, Ryan landed a tiny role as Kenny in his first film, *Frankenstein And Me*. Directed by Robert Tinnell, who had just finished directing another movie called *Kids Of The Round Table* (1997), *Frankenstein And Me* was shot on location in and around Montreal and starred Burt Reynolds and Louise Fletcher.

Set in a small town in the Mojave Desert, the plot centres on Earl Williams, a 12-year-old boy fixated with monsters. The screenplay, written by Richard Goudreau and David Sherman, based on a story by Robert Tinnell, concerns what happens when a monster-obsessed boy comes across a life-size monster resembling Frankenstein left behind in the street by a travelling carnival.

Earl spends the rest of the movie trying to get the monster to come to life. The film, known as *Frankenstein Et Moi* in

Canada, went straight to video in the US on 18 March 1997, having premiered at the Fantasporto Film Festival in Portugal in February 1997.

Returning to TV – and, as with all this work, it apparently came about through Ryan and his mother's pushing ahead, since Ryan is believed to have only signed on with an agent later – Ryan made a guest appearance in an episode of *The Adventures Of Shirley Holmes*, a Canadian mystery TV series running from 1996 to 1999. Conceived by Phil Meagher and Ellis Iddon, the show centred on the adventures of Sherlock Holmes' great-grand-niece, Shirley Holmes, who was played by Meredith Henderson.

Ryan appears as a character called Sean, in an episode titled 'The Case Of The Burning Building'. The episode, which didn't reach our TV screens until 7 May 1997, saw Shirley set on a trail to solve the mystery of who was causing a series of fires that had suddenly broken out.

Early in 1997, Ryan landed his biggest part to date – a permanent recurring role in a TV series called *Breaker High*. The Canadian teen show, created by Cori Stern and Laura Wegner, would run on TV from 15 September 1997 to 30 March 1998. Filmed in Burnaby, British Columbia, the show's premise was that *Breaker High* was a high school on board a cruise ship. The ship docked often, in various places, affording opportunities for different storylines. It was conceived to be a teen show that loosely aped the scenario of the cruise ship TV sitcom *The Love Boat*, which had enjoyed an incredibly successful run from 1977 to 1986.

Despite *Breaker High*'s school-on-the-sea concept, the show was mostly filmed in a warehouse. Apparently, there was only one day of actual shooting out to sea, so the crew could capture stock footage.

For his contract, Ryan was signed up to appear in the entire series as Sean Hanlon. His stint was to last for all 44 episodes of the show. The scale of such a contract made it clear that Ryan was starting to rack up enough credits to merit such a long-term commitment. In the opening credits, he received top billing, along with Rachel Wilson – both of their names flashed up onscreen simultaneously. Wilson played the part of Tamira Goldstein and, like Ryan, she had made a guest appearance in *Are You Afraid Of The Dark?*. Also top-billed in the cast were Terri Conn, who played Ashley Dupree, and Kyle Alisharan (Alex Pineda).

Ryan's character, Sean Hanlon, was meant to be the ladies' man of the show, but his attempts to play it cool with the girls mostly fell flat, making him seem laughable. Ryan approached playing him as if he were a throwback to a smooth-talking hipster from the 1950s – the kind of wise talker who could have been a member of the Rat Pack, such as Frank Sinatra, Dean Martin or Sammy Davis Jr. In reality, Sean always tries too hard and scares away the girls he's interested in.

In one scene, Sean is narcissistically dancing naked in front of a mirror when Tamira and Jimmy walk in unannounced and surprise him. He is at first bashful, then flashes Tamira a grin as if to say, 'Hey, check me out!' before he clocks that she's embarrassed and not at all impressed so instead covers himself up using a desktop computer. This is classic Sean

Hanlon – trying to be a tough guy before the girls, he ends up coming off as a narcissistic nerd.

In the loosest sense, Hanlon is the raw, un-manicured teenage version of Jacob Palmer, the seasoned veteran ladies' man Ryan would later play to such winning effect in *Crazy, Stupid, Love*.

Throughout the series, Ryan looks incredibly tall onscreen compared to his co-stars – heading for his 17th birthday, he was presumably getting close to his full height of 6'1". Watching the show, one can also see how he slowly gains confidence with the role as the series passes – the benefits of a recurring role snowballing as the episodes stack up. It's possible that prior to signing up for *Breaker High* he had found it hard to work in such an ad hoc way: the endless chopping and changing as he turned up to shoot one guest role after another may well have been at odds with his attention span, which meant that he never had the chance to get into character. However, with an entire series spread out before him, he was able to get a strong handle on Sean Hanlon and immerse himself in the character: as a result, he increasingly becomes the centre of the show as his mounting onscreen charisma shines ever brighter.

As it was Ryan's first recurring role and the series was a teen show, it is his equivalent of Michelle Williams' own recurring role in *Dawson's Creek*. Watching *Breaker High* and *Dawson's Creek*, it is hard to see that both would eventually wind up co-starring in an independent film with such gravitas as *Blue Valentine*.

Ryan's next part was as Tommy in a made-for-TV film

called *Nothing Too Good For A Cowboy*, which would go on to spawn a series of the same name. Directed by Kari Skogland and written by David Barlow and Charles Lazer, it was adapted from the book of the same name by Richmond P. Hobson Jr. The film, which concerns a rancher and a wealthy woman who fall in love across a social divide, starred Chad Willett, Sarah Chalke and Ted Atherton. The film would later premiere on TV in Canada on 4 January 1998.

Despite all these TV and film parts seemingly steering him towards a successful career as a TV actor, Ryan had itchy feet and wanted to change lanes and point himself towards a more ambitious film career. With his mother's blessing, Ryan left high school at the age of 17 and moved to Los Angeles, intending to take his acting career to the biggest stage of all.

CHAPTER SIX

STARTING OVER

If Ryan hadn't made that leap and left Canada for California, it's likely that he would have continued to move up the Canadian TV ladder. Yes, he had a long list of credits attached to his name now, but all of those credits firmly typecast him as a children's TV actor. To move into TV in the USA, and ideally film work, he knew he'd have to find a crack in a door and somehow sneak his way through.

Staying with friends he'd met through his career to date, and, with his list of credits to date, in particular that of Sean Hanlon on *Breaker High*, Ryan was able to find himself an agent. Through signing with that agent, he had opportunities.

His first break, early in 1998, saw him audition in Los Angeles, for the part of Hercules in a spin-off show called *Young Hercules*. The auditions were long-winded and he was excited when he finally made it to the last stages. When he learned that he had actually been chosen for the starring role, it felt like a landmark moment.

He would get to act in a TV show that would take him back to all those action movies he once adored, starring Sylvester Stallone and Arnold Schwarzenegger. His role would serve as a tip of the hat back to his younger self, just as being a Mouseketeer had been a nod to his love for Michael Jackson's music, his uncle Perry's Elvis Perry act, all those weddings and talent shows he performed at with his sister Mandi and his onetime ambition to become a professional dancer.

The contract he signed bound him to a run of 49 episodes, making this another long-term recurring role. It also meant the security of a long-running pay cheque. In every respect, it was a great break.

To shoot the series, though, Ryan would need to leave Los Angeles and relocate to New Zealand, where the show was to be made. With a budget of less than $20 million, it was decided that episodes would be filmed in blocks of four – with three different directors working on the series, who would all take turns in shooting these blocks.

Being only 17, thin and now standing at 6'1", Ryan had to train intensely to build up a credible physique for the part. This meant he needed to be initiated into intense martial arts training, which involved heavy gym rotation and also kung fu classes. Ryan told *The Insider* at the time about the preparation process, explaining, 'I've been doing some kung fu classes with Duncan Wong who taught Hercules [Kevin Sorbo] and Xena [Lucy Lawless]. He's been trying to get me up to speed, to where they're at. It's been a lot of fun. Even now I feel a lot more confident just walking on the street. I've seen every Bruce Lee movie ever made – that's my experience!'

Even after all that training, he was still too thin and gangly, which meant that the costume design department had to specially create his costume so that he looked bulkier in his upper torso than he actually did in real life.

At all times, Ryan was incredibly professional, no matter how challenging a scene. In one episode titled 'Forgery', he was meant to wear red contact lenses to give the impression that a run-in with Zeus had altered his character. The crew kept trying to put the contact lenses into his eyes and it was agonising, causing tears to stream. After 20 minutes of trying and failing to fit them, another member of the crew (who knew how contact lenses worked) pointed out that they were trying to fit them in Ryan's eyes back to front – which explained the searing discomfort it was causing the young actor. As soon as they fitted them correctly, the pain ceased. But before this, despite the agony of the contact lenses being incorrectly fitted, over and over, Ryan never once told them to stop or uttered a word of complaint.

Young Hercules made its debut on Fox Kids on 12 September 1998. Ryan's take on the young Hercules was confident and well played – his onscreen confidence was getting ever stronger. Ratings for the show were solid, though it would not be renewed for a second season.

Two months later, while out in New Zealand shooting later episodes of the show, Ryan turned 18 on 12 November 1998. Also around this time, while still on location, Ryan made a guest appearance in the accompanying, older, popular TV show *Hercules: The Legendary Journeys*, which had been on air since 1995. Starring Kevin Sorbo and Michael Hurst, the series followed a formula, riffing on the adventures of Greek divine hero Hercules. Ryan appeared in Episode 17, Season 5, titled 'The Academy' and played Zylus. It would later air on TV on 15 March 1999.

When he got back to Los Angeles, in early 1999, he signed up to appear in a TV series pilot called *The Unbelievables*. The show, which never made it past pilot stage and failed to go into development as a series, was meant to revolve around two superheroes, played by Corbin Bernsen and Tim Curry. In the pilot, Ryan was cast as Josh – a character intended to be the son of Corbin Bernsen's untitled character. Playing Tim Curry's also untitled superhero sidekick was Steve Carell, with whom Ryan would later work on *Crazy, Stupid, Love*. This Canadian production, shot in 1999, was written and directed by Ed Solomon, who had written for successful movies such as *Men In Black* and *Leaving Normal*, and TV shows like *Bill & Ted's Excellent Adventure*. Ryan later told *Glam* about how funny he found Steve Carell: 'When I first moved to LA I got this part in a pilot and he had a small part too. We didn't work together but he was so funny that I'd go to the set just to watch him work. One time he was so funny that the boom guy dropped the boom and had a laugh attack. I became a huge fan.'

Meanwhile, the final episode of *Young Hercules* aired on TV on 3 August 1999. Ryan later looked back on his time spent in New Zealand working on the show, describing the experience as follows to *Interview* magazine: 'I had a fake tan, leather pants. I was fighting imaginary monsters – they weren't really there, but I was acting like they were there.'

Harking back to the epiphany caused by his discovery of David Lynch's *Blue Velvet* and the music of Tom Waits and later films starring James Dean and Marlon Brando, Ryan saw no artistic merit to the work he was doing and, despite aspects of it that he obviously liked, in a deeper sense he wasn't fulfilled. He had it in his mind that he wanted to reshape himself as a film actor, which meant walking away from TV work and starting over in the more serious realm of feature filmmaking. From his work on *Breaker High* and *Young Hercules*, he knew that he worked best when he was allowed to luxuriate in a role, to familiarise himself with a character and this way of working also pointed him in the direction of feature film.

Once he had made this decision, nothing would stand in his way. As he later told *The Vancouver Sun*: 'I wanted to do films, have more time to sit with a character and to try to play different characters. So I just said, No more television.'

CHAPTER SEVEN

BREAKOUT

Ryan didn't walk straight into film work. This was likely down to his so far prolific background as a children's TV actor. Yes, he had had high-profile roles that would almost certainly have won him access to influential people in the film industry – his sustained stints in *The All New Mickey Mouse Club*, *Breaker High* and *Young Hercules* leading that list – but, just as easily, those roles could have pigeonholed him and undermined his bid to cross over into feature film.

As he later explained to *The New York Times*, he was well aware that the parts he had been playing were not the kind of work that would automatically propel him to serious film roles: 'It's very hard coming from kids' television to break the stigma. All you have is a VHS tape of you humping stuff on *The Mickey Mouse Club* and wearing fake tanner and fighting imaginary sphinxes.'

Despite this, he was as restless as ever and determined to push ahead. His perseverance paid off faster than he might have expected when he found out, in summer 1999, that he had landed a small part in a Disney film called *Remember The Titans*.

The film was to be directed by Boaz Yakin, who had most recently written and directed a movie called *A Price Above Rubies*, starring Renée Zellweger, Christopher Eccleston and Julianna Margulies. Written by Gregory Allen Howard, *Remember The Titans* had an estimated $30 million budget and was based on the true story of the T. C. Williams High School Titans football team.

Shot on location across Georgia, between 3 October and 14 December 1999, *Remember The Titans* was set in 1971 and told the story of Herman Boone, an African-American football coach (played by Denzel Washington), who, after two segregated Virginia schools – one white, one black – are closed and the students sent to the same school, becomes the coach of an integrated football team.

When Boone takes over coaching the team from Coach Bill Yoast (Will Patton), his appointment enrages some of the town's white inhabitants because now, not only is the team integrated, but it also has an African-American coach.

Ryan was hired to play Alan Bosley, a member of the football team. His prime scene takes place in a locker room, where his character has to first dance to a Country & Western number and then sing along with and dance to the 1967 Marvin Gaye and Tammi Terrell soul classic 'Ain't No Mountain High Enough'. He handles the scene effortlessly, no doubt calling on his background as a singing and dancing Mouseketeer. Watching it today, one sees an actor lighting up the screen with energy, ambition and a determination to be noticed.

The film gave Ryan a supreme taste of where he wanted to be permanently: the opportunity to sign up to play an interesting character, to prepare for the role, to spend time in character and develop the part, to deliver a confident thought-through performance. This was what he wanted, not the episodic formula of a TV series.

Hungry to cross over for good after making *Remember The Titans*, he was now on the lookout for a role that he could really sink his teeth into; a showcase for his talents, where he could explode his potential. The reality was that while *Remember The Titans* seemed like a big break – and it was in that it gave him that proverbial foot in the door into the fiercely competitive realm of Hollywood – his part had been tiny. Though it would have felt like a quick and giant step towards where he wanted to be, it must have also felt like a step back, having worked his way up to first co-starring in *Breaker High* and then the starring role in *Young Hercules*. What he wanted now was to catch up with his ambitions, which meant bulldozing his way into film as quickly as possible and rocketing his reputation right back to the same parallel high profile – only as a film actor.

As had happened when he moved to Los Angeles and arrived rapidly at his *Young Hercules* break, this time he didn't have to wait long either. Several of Ryan's actor friends were preparing to audition for a film part. The role was that of a young man called Danny Balint, a modern-day Neo-Nazi holding on tightly to a profound, intense secret: he is Jewish. He told *bbc.co.uk* what happened next: 'I was helping one of them with his lines. As I read it, I realized I wanted to play Danny real bad. So I begged to get an audition. I was lucky that Henry [Bean] fitted me in as his last appointment.'

Ryan just scraped the chance to audition, since Bean and his producer and casting director were planning on heading back to New York right after he would read for them.

The screenplay for *The Believer* was written by Henry Bean, who was also intending to direct, and was loosely inspired by a true story that had haunted him for many years. This story, which took place in 1965, was the bizarre tale of a high-ranking New York area Ku Klux Klan member discovered to be Jewish by a reporter for *The New York Times*.

The reporter met the man (Daniel Burros) after he was arrested at a Brooklyn meeting of the Ku Klux Klan. After having to sit through a lengthy anti-Semitic diatribe from Burros, the reporter waited for his moment and then asked how on earth he could believe and say such things, given that he himself was a Jew. Stunned, Burros furiously denied what the reporter had said. The reporter, who had done his detective work, kept pushing Burros, saying that it was true since he had met the rabbi who had bar mitzvah'd Burros and therefore had proof.

The meeting ended with Burros telling the reporter that, if he printed this story, he would kill himself. *The New York Times* went ahead and published the exposé. Within hours, Burros had shot himself at a Pennsylvania camp used by his Neo-Nazi group.

Bean first heard this story circa 1975 and it stayed with him thereafter, coming back to him from time to time, as unfathomable tales tend to do. In time, he ended up learning more about the details when he bought a copy of the 1967 book *One More Victim: The Life and Death of a Jewish Nazi*, by Abe Rosenthal and Arthur Gelb. Eventually, he sat down and started developing a screenplay with Mark Jacobson loosely based on the story of Daniel Burros but recast in modern-day New York.

At this time, Bean was best known for having co-written Chantal Akerman's 1986 film *Golden Eighties* and having penned outright Mike Figgis' *Internal Affairs* (1990) and Bill Duke's 1992 movie *Deep Cover*. He has said what particularly interested him in Burros' conflict was the battle to contain his secret, while on occasion seemingly going out of his way to drop hints that he was Jewish. Bean elaborated on why this resonated so deeply with him in an interview with *Moviemaker.com*: 'The movie is about someone who wants to be a Jew and a Nazi at the same time. He wants to be a living contradiction. Once I had that, it was the organizing principle of everything. He wants to be pulled apart by opposing appetites.'

To add layering to the screenplay, Bean drew on his own Jewish identity and upbringing in what he told *The Jewish Journal* was a 'very, very Reform home' and also what he had learned about Judaism from his wife, the screenwriter Leora Barish – who wrote the screenplay to the hit 1985 Madonna vehicle *Desperately Seeking Susan*, and had also co-written *Golden Eighties* with Bean – who was the daughter of a

Conservative rabbi. By the time he was writing the screenplay, Bean had stepped closer to a religious life himself and was now not only keeping a kosher home but also attending a Conservative minyan, a public gathering for Jewish worship, made credible, as per the instruction of the Talmud, by its consisting of a quorum of 10 Jewish males over the age of 13.

To help think through the screenplay, Bean had also trialled the story in the form of a short film called *The Jewish Nazi* in which the lead role of Danny Balint was played by Judah Lazarus, a local Orthodox Jew known to him. Thanks to this experiment, Bean had a very clear picture of the kind of actor he was after for the feature-length version: he wanted someone who was in his mid- to late twenties, who would look neither obviously Jewish nor too obviously not Jewish, with a solid working understanding of both Judaism and Hebrew.

Bean had also made the short film so he had a calling card of sorts to introduce the project to potential backers, but, even with this illustrative vehicle, he was finding it hard to attract interest. He was mostly getting the same feedback – that the topic was too hot, too complex and too contentious. However, the nervousness of potential backers only served to encourage him more, and the less support he found, the more determined he became to make the film to the extent that he committed to personally putting up $500,000 of his own money – funds he and his wife had amassed from their combined screenwriting work.

With at least that budget, Bean was able to secure two key cast members: Billy Zane and Theresa Russell, who would respectively play the parts of Curtis Zampf and Lina

Moebius. But, no matter how hard he thought about it, he could not conjure up an actor suitable to handle the part of Danny Balint.

After a round of auditions in New York failed to find him the right person, Bean was faced with other headaches, namely negative reactions to the title of the film, which was still pencilled in as *The Jewish Nazi*. To try to smooth the flow of the project, he changed the title to *The Believer* to make it sound more approachable and also to make it easier to scout potential filming locations. If they wanted to shoot film scenes in a synagogue, he imagined having a title like *The Jewish Nazi* would make getting permission difficult.

After the casting sessions in New York failed to source them their Danny Balint, Bean, producer Christopher Roberts and head of casting, Adrienne Stern, decided to set up a casting session on the West Coast. If they couldn't find their man in New York, maybe they would do so in Los Angeles.

The auditions didn't fare much better in Los Angeles, though. It seemed their specifications for Danny were too elusive, that every actor who walked into the audition just didn't have the fit they were after. But then, just as they started to get a sinking feeling, a young actor they'd never heard of got in touch and all but begged to audition for the part. As far as they were concerned, if he was that keen, they should see him, even if he was coming out of nowhere. They told him that they would see him, but only if he could come after they'd seen the last actor at the end of the formal, scheduled casting sessions. No matter what, Ryan would be there.

Although Ryan arrived crackling with excitement, with

nerves, with energy, Bean and Roberts' first impression of him wasn't a good one. They said that, when he turned up, he seemed to be wrong for the part in every conceivable way. For a start, he was only 19 years old – and they were, as we know, looking for an actor somewhere between his mid- and late twenties. The next thing that jarred dissonantly with their brief was his height – here was a very tall, very skinny actor, who stood at 6'1". And then, on top of that, he had short, messy, dyed blond hair. No part of this picture suggested that he could handle a role in which he'd need to look somewhat Jewish, but not obviously so. Instead of fulfilling that look, he appeared more like a gangly, blond-haired Scandinavian giant.

Ryan then sat down on the floor and sprawled out and gave his audition this way. Inside, the team must have been groaning – here was this 6'1"- tall, bleach-blond 19-year-old, gangly unknown actor lying on the floor, surely about to give an audition as ill-suited as his appearance. But, no, Ryan pulled out an ace as he gave his reading and everybody sat up: there was something to this actor.

As he tore into the screenplay's themes and Danny's story and ideology, he came off as fragile and sensitive, explosive and simmering. In the back of his mind, Ryan was worried that Bean and his team would see his children's TV work as a major negative and would regard his fake tan and period-costume romping as Young Hercules as too cheesy for him to be able to cross over to this particular role with the necessary credibility.

But Bean was thinking the opposite: he wanted an unknown actor to star in his film. He didn't want his audiences to make associations; he wanted them to forget that it was a film and Danny Balint was being played by an actor; he wanted to shoot in a documentary style so that audiences would be completely immersed in a sense of disturbed reality and lose any sense of it not being real.

The decisive moment came not during the audition itself, but afterwards. Yes, Ryan's reading had impressed everybody but he was to do one final thing, off the cuff, that would seal the deal. When the audition had ended and Ryan was preparing to leave, he spoke privately with Adrienne Stern and told her that he wanted to personally apologise to her for saying such horrible things at the audition. He said he had found it hard to say such hateful, anti-Semitic things and he wanted her to know that he was upset at having said such things out loud.

She was astonished by this – no other actor who had tried out for the part had said anything like this. They had read their lines or improvised and left. But this was different: here was this sensitive, vulnerable young man, with intense eyes, apologising for the anti-Semitic vitriol he had been expected to say at the audition.

After she talked it over with Bean and Roberts, they agreed that, in this scenario, Ryan had unintentionally projected the exact inner conflict they wanted Danny Balint to project onscreen.

What had happened, of course, was that Ryan, having been raised in a Mormon family, had been taught a reverence for all faiths and, during the audition, he had found it very difficult to assault another religion, another faith, so violently and with such bigoted, demented hatred. This had fired up a conflict in him, which to his amazement landed him the part of Danny Balint.

It took a while for the news to sink in: he had landed his first leading role in a feature film. He had achieved his dramatic shortcut and made the leap to a high level and profile within the film industry.

It's important to remember that he was still only 19 years old and that, in the span of seven years, he had managed to beat 15,000 hopefuls to become Canada's first Mouseketeer. He had also climbed the ladder of children's TV to find first a recurring, co-starring role on *Breaker High*, followed by a starring role in *Young Hercules* and then, after shifting his ambitions towards film work, he had launched his film acting career in what was soon to become a hit Denzel Washington vehicle. Now, as if by magic, he had turned up to an audition at the last possible moment, wowed everyone involved in the casting and landed his first starring role in a feature film. Suddenly, it seemed as if, wherever Ryan directed his ambition, he was able to quickly storm his way to success.

CHAPTER EIGHT

RESEARCH AND CHARACTER BUILDING

Once Ryan was signed up for *The Believer*, Henry Bean asked him to travel to New York so that he could immerse himself in the milieu of his character and get a handle on the life and world that Bean had written about in his screenplay.

This was to be the first time that Ryan would prepare for a role in the manner of Marlon Brando, Robert De Niro and the other Method actors – by throwing himself into the work, building his sense of character and trying to get as comfortable in Danny's shoes as he possibly could before playing him.

For research, he would ride the New York subway for hours at a time, integrating himself with the city, its rhythm and the people on the trains. Bean also introduced him to Judah Lazarus, who had played Danny Balint in the short film, and Lazarus took him inside the life of New York Orthodox

Judaism, showing him around Jewish neighbourhoods, explaining how the communities worked and how the rituals of Judaism functioned.

The degree to which Ryan prepared for the role – and this kind of detailed preparation was to become standard for him from now on – has led many people to assume that he is a Method actor and follows that school of acting. However, somewhat remarkably, he has never formally studied acting and certainly not Method acting. He goes about preparing for a role in the way that most Method actors do, but he has kept a humble line about this process, preferring not to dress it up in any professional framework.

Taking things deeper, Ryan set about learning Hebrew and dedicated himself to reading the Torah every morning. While studying Hebrew and the Torah, he would also visit synagogues as often as possible, soaking up every last detail of the services, the people attending them, the demeanour of the rabbis. He rode the tension of sitting in during services, his secret being that he wasn't Jewish – this helped him build the sense of having a secret and what that felt like within a strict religious community.

As Bean finalised casting and financing and the film geared up to go into production, he was ever more convinced that Ryan's religious upbringing made him perfect for the part. He had always felt it was crucial that Danny be played by an actor with an understanding of what it means to live within a religious framework, and not only had Ryan lived this way but he also understood the life implicitly.

To help Ryan feel as confident as possible about speaking

Hebrew, Bean's wife, Leora Barish, personally dedicated herself to tutoring him. Ryan told the BBC, 'She spent many, many hours working on my Hebrew. I can still hear her in my head and when I watch the film I can hear the difference.'

It's almost impossible not to wonder whether the sessions with Barish reminded Ryan of his year of home schooling and if that was why he responded so quickly and well to what she was teaching him.

By the time they were ready to shoot, the film had a $1.5 million budget. If the financial side of things was now in a more confident place, Ryan, on the other hand, was feeling less so. As had happened when he started work on *The All New Mickey Mouse Club Show*, he suddenly suffered an attack of confidence. He was concerned about meeting the expectations of Henry Bean and everybody else involved in the making of the film. However, he was in no doubt that he was on the right career path now since he loved every second of the research, of the character building. After all, this was what he had dreamed of: the opportunity and time to play a part in which he could lose himself and develop the character as fully as possible.

He challenged any doubts he might have had with the intuitive knowledge that, when reading for the role, he had the conviction that he loved and wanted this part more than any other actor who might stand – or lie on the floor – before the filmmakers.

When the film wrapped at the end of July 2000, it was clear that the team had been right in their choice of Ryan to play the part of Danny. He brought a phenomenal intensity to the role. Bean's hunch that Ryan's Mormon background took him into the part of Danny proved right, as he later told *Nerve*, 'I thought, "I have to cast a Jewish kid", but I found that when I auditioned, Jewish kids didn't know much more than anybody else. Ryan understood something about religion. Mormonism is very demanding, and it isolates you the way Judaism isolates you. And he got all that.'

Onscreen, he crackles with the intensity of Robert De Niro in Martin Scorsese's *Taxi Driver*, Gary Oldman in Phil Joanou's *State of Grace*, Christopher Walken in *The Deer Hunter* or Joaquin Phoenix in *We Own The Night*.

Alongside such an evident onscreen maturity, which far outstripped his actual years, Ryan also brought a boyish vulnerability to the role, which together would go on to become one of his trademarks – the uncanny ability to appear onscreen as both very young and very old at the same time.

Ryan also appeared incredibly tender in certain scenes with Summer Phoenix – the sister of River Phoenix, Rain Phoenix and Joaquin Phoenix – who plays the part of Carla Moebius. At the time, Ryan was 19, while Summer was 21.

Drained and exhilarated, he went back to Los Angeles after he had finished shooting the film. He had pulled it off – his first leading role in a feature film.

On 23 September 2000, *Remember The Titans* premiered at the Rose Bowl in Pasadena, California. Powered by positive reviews, the film opened at cinemas on 1 October 2000, taking $20,905,831 over its opening weekend. It would go on to gross $115,654,751 worldwide, meaning that the first serious feature Ryan appeared in had turned out to be a significant commercial success.

No doubt building on his part as a football player in *Remember The Titans*, he was then cast in another role as a football player, this time in another independent film.

The Slaughter Rule was co-written and co-directed by twin brothers Alex and Andrew J. Smith, and had an estimated budget of $500,000. Previously, the twins had written and directed a short film called *The Keening* in 1999 and were now making the step up to shoot their first feature film.

In this coming-of-age drama, Ryan plays Roy Chutney, a James Dean-esque character, who after losing his father is dropped from his beloved football team. Distant with his mother (played by Kelly Lynch), grieving for his father and cut out of the football team that had given him a sense of validation, belonging and purpose, he seeks a connection with a barmaid called Skyla (Clea DuVall). He then meets Gideon Ferguson, a mysterious, marginalised local (played by David Morse), who invites Roy to join his unofficial six-man high school football team. As he and Roy become ever closer, Roy begins to wonder if the rumours about Gideon being gay are true.

The film was shot quickly, in just 20 days, on location in Montana, over November and December 2000. In the middle of the shoot, Ryan turned 20 – with so much work already under his belt, it seemed hard to believe that he was only just checking out of his teens.

By the end of that year, he was ready to push forward and take things to the next level. With a growing momentum, he was enjoying being part of the commercial success of *Remember The Titans* and waited eagerly to see how his performance in *The Believer* would be received when it premiered at the Sundance Film Festival in January 2001.

CHAPTER NINE

MURDER BY NUMBERS

The year 2001 opened with Ryan poised to play his most high-profile role to date. He had landed the part of Richard Haywood in a psychological thriller called *Murder By Numbers*. The film was set to star Sandra Bullock, which meant that he was about to have the opportunity to work opposite an internationally renowned actress.

Bullock, who was 36 at the time the film went into production, was riding high after appearing in movies such as *Miss Congeniality*, *28 Days*, *Practical Magic*, *Hope Floats*, *While You Were Sleeping* and *Speed*. Working alongside her was a major step up and Ryan knew it. This was another huge break. His career as a film actor was moving faster than he could ever have dreamed of – all those blink-and-you-could-miss-them TV guest roles were but a distant memory.

As he prepared for his new role, *The Believer* premiered at the Sundance Film Festival on 19 January 2001 and, to the delight of Henry Bean, Leora Barish, Christopher Roberts and Ryan himself, was awarded the Grand Jury Prize – Dramatic. The prize was incredible news because it generated an instant buzz about the film. It was also a tremendous validation for Ryan, whose performance was singled out for its mesmerising rage and eerie gentleness.

As news of the win spread about the media, overnight, his name was bumped up onto the Hollywood map and, with it, he had taken another important step towards fully realising his goal of shaking off his Mouseketeer/children's TV and film actor past and re-announcing himself as a serious film actor. He later recalled this sudden jump up in his status in an interview with the *Guardian*, saying, 'I went to Sundance and when I left I had a career and I had choice. People talked to me as if I was an artist, and I tried to act smart and pretend to be one.'

Usually, if an independent film wins the Grand Jury Prize at Sundance, as *The Believer* did, the award fairly automatically segues into a flurry of distribution offers. However, things had never been straightforward with this particular project and they would not become any more straightforward now.

There were plenty of distributors who saw the merits of the film, but they were all nervous about it becoming a work that courted controversy, especially from Jewish organisations, which would spell box-office poison for the project. Although this was 2001, plenty of distributors remembered all too clearly the damaging controversy that had dogged Martin Scorsese's 1988 movie *The Last Temptation of Christ* and no

o award nominations just yet for a young Ryan Gosling in his debut role... as a
Mouseketeer in the Disney Channel's *Mickey Mouse Club*.   © *Everett Collection/ Rex Features*

Above left: Man's best friend: A fresh faced Ryan with his puppy George in 2001.

Above right: ...And not so fresh faced: 22-year-old Ryan leaving the *Murder by Number* premiere after-party in 2002.

Below: Youthful Ryan in a London cinema for the *Brotherhood of the Wolf* Film Gala in 2001.

A musical soul.

Above left: Strumming away at the *Animal Avengers* charity launch in 2001 (Club Vinyl, Hollywood).

© Getty Images

Above right: Ryan AKA Baby Goose rocking the bass at FYF Fest 2010 in rock band *Dead Man's Bones*.

© Getty Images

Below: Singing and playing the ukulele live to the nation on *Jimmy Kimmel Live!* in 2011.

© Getty Images

An early glimpse of the classic Ryan Gosling half-smile. © *Munawar Hosain/Rex Featur*

yan hits the red carpet with American sweetheart, co-star and then girlfriend Sandra
ullock at the 55th Cannes Film Festival 2002.

Above left: Ryan picks up the 'Male Star of Tomorrow' gong for his lead role in *The Notebook* at the ShoWest Awards 2004 (Paris Hotel, Las Vegas). © *Startraks photos/ Rex Feature*

Above right: Recreating the iconic kiss from *The Notebook* with Rachel McAdams at th 2005 MTV movie awards.
© *Getty Imag*

Below: Surfs up at the Teen Choice Awards, where the couple clean up in the 'Movie Chemistry, Liplock and Love Scene' categories.
© *Getty Imag*

bove left: To get an authentic 'documentary style' *Blue Valentine*, Ryan hefted heavy
ates up and down a five-storey building, even when the camera wasn't rolling!

© *Charles Sykes/Rex Features*

bove right: Work hard, play hard: tubing at the cast party in Utah, after some
ruelling filming. © *Getty Images*

elow: Hitting the red carpet at Hollywood's AFI Fest 2010 for a screening of
lue Valentine. © *Getty Images*

Family time: Ryan arrives
the Oscars awards ceremo
in 2007 flanked by siste
Mandi and mother Donn

© Sipa Press/Rex Featur

one wanted to acquire rights to a film that could open to mounting protests outside cinema doors.

To try to address the matter head on, Bean decided to arrange a screening for a rabbi who is regularly consulted by Hollywood when it requires guidance on films or projects with Jewish themes or issues that require expert authentication or clarification. The rabbi agreed to offer feedback and gathered together a small circle of colleagues for the screening. After Bean gave a brief introduction to the film, its origins and its message, the rabbi and his team sat back and watched.

According to an article that later appeared in *The New York Times*, the rabbi did not provide positive feedback. The newspaper quoted him as saying, 'I watched it with eight or nine staff members. It's not for us to say what kind of films people should make. But we all agreed that pedagogically, *The Believer* didn't work.'

The rabbi was reported to have been particularly troubled by the scene where Danny and his cohorts go to a synagogue with a plan to desecrate the Torah. *JWeekly* quoted him as saying, 'That scene alone could be a primer for anti-Semitism.'

Although there is no evidence whatsoever to suggest that the rabbi not liking the film affected its chances of receiving offers of distribution, it was obviously disappointing for Bean and everybody connected with the project to receive under-whelming feedback from such an influential figurehead in the Los Angeles Jewish community.

In the end, despite the Sundance award, successive distributors passed on acquiring rights to the movie, giving Bean one disappointment after another. Finally, he signed a deal that would see the work premiere on Showtime, the then popular cable channel, known at the time for going to bat for films perceived to be difficult. Within the agreement, there was a plan for Showtime to premiere the film later that year, in the autumn.

As Bean battled against the odds, Ryan was busy getting used to life with a new companion. He had acquired a dog who he named George. Why the name George, he has never said. He has also never revealed what species of dog, but most reports refer to George as being a mutt.

From then on, George and Ryan would be inseparable and there are countless photos in existence of Ryan with George. He apparently takes George with him when he shoots films on location and has even been known on occasion to take the dog on TV with him when he appears on talk shows.

On 27 February 2001, Ryan began work on *Murder By Numbers*. The film began life as a project backed by Castle Rock Entertainment and told the story of two privileged, disturbed high school teenagers, who set out to plan, perform and achieve the perfect murder.

With Ryan cast as Richard Haywood, the part of the other student, Justin Pendleton, was to be played by Michael Pitt, who, like Ryan, had first made his name on TV, with his recurring role as Henry Parker in *Dawson's Creek*. In *Murder By Numbers*, Pitt's Pendleton has a fascination with, and expert knowledge of forensic science, while Ryan's Haywood is one of the most popular students at their high school and, in effect, Pendleton's sidekick.

After the pair murder their first victim – a woman chosen at random – Pendleton masterminds the leaving of premeditated traces of evidence in a bid to pin the crime on their high school janitor/pot dealer, played by Sean Penn's brother Chris. With locals terrified by the murder, Detective Cassie Mayweather (Sandra Bullock) is put on the case. Haunted by a horrific event in her past, Mayweather investigates and suspects the boys of planning and executing the murder. As she intuitively closes in on them, accompanied by a new partner, Sam Kennedy (played by Ben Chaplin), a game of cat and mouse begins.

The script was by Tony Gayton, who also wrote *Salton Sea* (released simultaneously with *Murder By Numbers*). Prior to this, Gayton had penned the script for a documentary called *Athens GA, Inside Out* (1987), which looked at the artistic scene spearheaded by the band R.E.M. in Athens, a small town in the Southern state of Georgia.

Sandra Bullock became attached to the project after she was sent the script by Castle Rock Entertainment. She loved the story, feeling it had the content and tone of an old-fashioned thriller in the vein of a classic Alfred Hitchcock film. She expressed interest at the same time as Castle Rock received the same positive response from director Barbet Schroeder, to whom they had also sent the script.

What happened next was that Bullock and Schroeder met and went away from their meeting mutually very excited to make the film. Indeed, Bullock was so committed that she also signed on as executive producer.

Of the shoot itself, Schroeder later told *bbc.co.uk* that he loved every second of working with Ryan and Michael Pitt, saying, 'Every ten years there is a new generation of actors.

Now is the time for the changing of the guard, and this is a movie where I had the opportunity to cast two people [Ryan and Pitt] who I bet will be the actors of tomorrow.' His prediction would prove to be spot on.

The film, which had a budget of $50 million, was shot at a studio in Los Angeles and on location throughout Los Angeles and Los Angeles County, with some scenes shot in other parts of California – for instance, Morro Bay and San Luis Obispo.

Sandra Bullock apparently enjoyed learning more about forensics for her part as she mentioned in an interview with *IGN*: 'Forensics I've always found absolutely fascinating. Anything to do with clues. And checking things out and solving.' To authenticate the film's intense focus on forensics, experts from that field were on set during the film to counsel on scenes. Bullock told *IGN* she loved this aspect of the shoot, 'We had such great forensics experts working with us... We had this woman who was a blood expert. Oh that's exciting. The splatter, the consistency, whether it's been cut.'

By the time the film wrapped on 21 May 2001, many actors might have considered taking a break, but Ryan, even with three films queued for release – *The Believer*, *The Slaughter Rule* and *Murder By Numbers* – was already hungry for his next part.

CHAPTER TEN

THE
OUTSIDER

On 6 September 2001, Henry Bean and the cast of *The Believer* were in Los Angeles for the telefilm premiere at the Directors Guild of America. In a very casual photograph taken at the event, Ryan, wearing a blazer, shirt and trousers, stands with his arm around Summer Phoenix, while Henry Bean, standing to Ryan's right, has his arm in turn around Theresa Russell. The photo speaks volumes of the camaraderie that had developed about the cast and crew during the making of the film.

The telefilm premiere was designed to generate advance buzz for the premiere on Showtime on 30 September, a date that had been chosen because it fell just after the Jewish holiday of Rosh Hashanah had come to an end. The channel believed premiering the movie then would encourage immediate debate. Everything was set for the film to finally have a wide audience. Ryan and everyone connected to the project waited for their efforts to finally go out into the world. But then, five days after the Los Angeles premiere, the terrorist attacks of 9/11 were unleashed and rocked the world.

On account of *The Believer*'s plotline – in particular, Danny's planting of the bomb in the synagogue – Showtime had no choice but to act out of sensitivity and postpone the 30 September premiere. Soon afterwards, they rescheduled the premiere for March 2002, the thinking being that the screening should once again be timed to coincide with another Jewish holiday: Passover.

Even if Ryan was likely becoming frustrated at the long wait for *The Believer* to be properly released, his attention was by now elsewhere. He had read a script called *The United States Of Leland* and fallen in love with it. This was not a large budget film like *Murder By Numbers*. Instead, it was a return to the small-budget, high-intensity, passionate scale of *The Believer*.

The United States Of Leland had been written by Matthew Ryan Hoge, who also intended to direct. It was Hoge's first feature film and his second effort as writer-director. His first film, a short called *Self Storage*, was released in 1999.

Ryan signed up to play the lead part of Leland P. Fitzgerald, an emotionally detached and troubled 16-year-old boy who, seemingly without motive, suddenly and violently stabs his girlfriend's autistic brother to death.

The film would focus on Leland's incarceration in juvenile hall and the relationship that unfolds there between Leland and a teacher/aspiring writer, Pearl Madison (played by Don

Cheadle), who sees Leland's story, as the teenager gradually confides in him around their timetabled classes, as inspiration for a potential book. As Madison and Leland become closer, Leland's celebrated novelist father (Kevin Spacey) and the family of the murdered boy join in the process of trying to make sense of what Leland has done.

When Ryan read the script, what he especially liked was the idea that Leland was detached from the world, from other people, and he was excited, as an actor, by the challenge to find a way to translate that emotional disconnect to a cinema screen.

Hoge had written the screenplay after working as a teacher in a juvenile detention centre. Helping the teenage inmates learn to express themselves creatively, he had often been struck by how entirely normal these young men seemed – despite the reasons they had been incarcerated. He had taken the teaching job because it kept him busy for several days per week, paid reasonably well and allowed him to spend the rest of the week writing. Essentially, it enabled him to set himself up in Los Angeles and pursue his filmmaking dreams.

He didn't, however, expect the job to be so intense and to offer him a story on a plate – a scenario he, of course, channelled through the character of Pearl Madison, the teacher in the film, who is criticised by those around him, including Leland's father, for using his son's tragic story as inspiration for his own writing.

When Hoge began shopping his finished screenplay around, he received plenty of positive feedback, but no producer wanted to take on the project. To his surprise, the script ended up in the offices of actor Kevin Spacey's production company, Trigger Street Productions. Spacey personally connected with the story and proposed not only that he should produce the film, but also that he should play the part of Leland's father – a double fantasy scenario for Hoge.

Hoge saw Ryan's job as the hardest of all, for he would have to give Leland an onscreen power and charisma, based on very little. The elliptical nature of Leland's story meant that he would need to communicate a lot of his character in a non-verbal way if the audience was to connect with him and, in turn, with the film.

To set Ryan off in the right direction, Hoge sent him home during pre-production with copies of two books: J.D. Salinger's 1951 novel *The Catcher In the Rye* and Albert Camus' 1942 novel *The Outsider*. Both books have narrators who feel disconnected and shut out of the world and yet, on the inside, are raging with feeling: Hoge wanted Ryan to play Leland this way. He especially wanted him to pay attention to the icy, detached tone of the narrator's voice in Camus' *The Outsider*.

Ryan's preparation also involved the building of physical tics that would give Leland a strong presence onscreen. Part of this process saw him experiment with his facial expression until he arrived at a place where he would play Leland with his bottom lip heavily emphasised, as if it were a buffer against a world he could not cope with.

As Ryan firmed up these physical details, Hoge was intrigued to watch him change his posture, his voice and subtle facial expressions as rehearsals gathered pace. What he had learned to do while preparing for *The Believer*, he was now doing with confidence and that meant no detail was left unexplored, no question about Leland left unanswered.

To play his character in such an internalised way, he would need to know him absolutely, to have drawn him out and fully realised him; to peel back the detail and, via a process of subtraction, arrive at a point where he could communicate the essence of Leland with a mere look.

Around this time, Ryan told Hoge that the bottom-lip detail was a technique he had come up with in order to let the audience know that he would not be inviting them into Leland's world but instead telling them to stay out – it was this kind of actor's shorthand that helped Ryan play Leland with the disconnected, buried-beneath-a-layer-of-ice tone of Camus' *The Outsider*.

To get in the mindset of Leland's relationship with his teacher, Ryan accompanied Hoge to the juvenile detention centre where he worked as a teacher. There, he spent days observing Hoge at work and how he interacted with the inmates. He sat in during classes and watched Hoge teach the inmates how to express themselves using dance, writing and literature. Being able to watch the inmates and to study how they behaved proved invaluable because it gave him first-hand insights into what it might be like to wake up in Leland's shoes.

Once everything was set to go, the film was shot during February 2002 in Los Angeles. To authenticate his role as Leland's father, Kevin Spacey would rather cleverly watch the dailies (raw footage shot that day) of Ryan's scenes, pick up on how Ryan played Leland and then absorb some of the tics and character traits and import them to Leland's father's character for scenes he was shooting – an ingenious way for him to draw reference to the idea that a son always learns from and imitates his father's persona.

By the time *The United States Of Leland* shoot had wrapped, *The Believer*, at long last, premiered on Showtime on 8 March 2002 at 8pm. To promote the screening, a significant article about the film appeared in *The New York Times*, pegged on the premiere. In the piece, Ryan offered his take on Danny Balint and the film, saying, 'He [Danny] loved Judaism so much that he felt weak because of his need for it.'

Despite all the controversy that had happened along the way, the Showtime premiere helped generate mostly positive reviews for both the film and, in particular, Ryan. *The New York Times* had this to say: 'No doubt the movie wowed them at Sundance because of its unnerving combination of willful sacrilege and religious desire wrapped in the bristling package of Mr. Gosling's muscular performance', while *Rolling Stone* zoomed in on Ryan's performance, gushing, 'Gosling gives a great, dare-anything performance that will be talked of for ages.'

Meanwhile, back in January, *The Believer* had also received multiple nominations at the 17th Independent Spirit Awards – in the categories of Best Screenplay and Best First Feature. Summer Phoenix had also been nominated in the Best Supporting Female category and Ryan was nominated for the Best Male Lead.

For Ryan, the nomination marked the first time his acting skills had been acknowledged in any major industry awards.

He had been nominated for the award in competition with Brian Cox for *L.I.E.*, Jake Gyllenhaal (*Donnie Darko*), Tom Wilkinson (*In the Bedroom*) and John Cameron Mitchell for *Hedwig And The Angry Inch*.

On 23 March, the Independent Spirit Awards were announced. Sadly, none of *The Believer*'s nominations materialised into actual awards. Ryan ended up losing out to Tom Wilkinson and *In The Bedroom*.

Several weeks later, on 16 April, *Murder By Numbers* premiered in New York. Ryan turned up for the premiere dressed down and unassuming, wearing a brown jacket, a brown shirt, black trousers and black shoes. He had not yet assumed the stylish, dapper appearance that would become his trademark at film premieres or awards ceremonies. Here, he seemed to be deliberately dressing in an understated way, as if he was trying to manage the already incredible level of attention he'd attracted to himself at such a young age.

The film opened in cinemas on 19 April and took $9,307,394 over its opening weekend. It would go on to gross a total of $56,714,147. To drive up European interest, it also screened at the Cannes Film Festival out of competition on 24 May. Ryan and Sandra Bullock flew out to Cannes for the screening and posed together for photographs.

It was around now that the closeness that had developed between Ryan and Sandra Bullock while they were shooting *Murder By Numbers* turned into an alleged romance. The relationship is reported to have not started on set, as romances between co-stars often tend to do, but when the pair were out on the film's promotional trail.

People magazine describe their very private coming together as follows: 'She [Sandra Bullock] quietly begins dating co-star Ryan Gosling, who is 16 years younger than Bullock. The two date for more than a year, but keep their relationship very private.'

Although photographs of the pair at the Cannes Film Festival do appear to suggest a shared chemistry and mutual happiness that transcends an actor and actress happy to be in the South of France promoting a film they've worked on together, neither ever publicly acknowledged that they were dating. All we know is that multiple sources speculate that they were a couple for approximately a year.

Since then, neither has acknowledged having dated the other by name, which leaves detail on their alleged relationship scarce at best. Having said that, in an interview with *The Times* in 2011, Ryan did allude to two defining romantic relationships in his life, saying, 'I had two of the greatest girlfriends of all time. I haven't met anybody who could top them.' This comment was widely interpreted to have been about Sandra Bullock and someone, who at this time, was to become a future girlfriend – Rachel McAdams, whom Ryan would meet while making *The Notebook*.

As to the details of Ryan's relationship with Sandra Bullock, we can only imagine how they came together, whether Ryan was in awe of Bullock's career and fame, whether they attended parties together or kept the relationship very private, how deep their connection was, whether their significant age difference was an issue or something they talked about often, what exactly it was that they had in common and so on.

From what little we know since, the couple did apparently juggle geography, since Bullock's home at this time was in Texas and Ryan was living in Los Angeles, which meant that, between the distance and their combined work schedules, their actual time together during that year was presumably cut to a minimum.

A month later, in sharp contrast to the box-office takings of *Murder By Numbers*, *The Believer* opened in the US on 19 May 2002 at four cinemas and took a total of $26,263 over the opening weekend despite unanimously positive reviews, which singled out Ryan's breakthrough performance as electrifying.

The critic Roger Ebert succinctly captured the remarkable career transformation that Ryan had strategised for himself when he landed this part, in writing in his review for the *Chicago Sun Times*: 'Ryan Gosling (who, incredibly, was a Mouseketeer contemporary of Britney Spears) is at 22 a powerful young actor.'

The point here is that a film critic as respected as Ebert was wrestling with the extraordinary process of reinvention that Ryan had achieved here – which was that of a child star on children's TV completely overhauling his identity and re-announcing himself as an incredibly serious and talented young actor.

It's a depressing reality that many child stars cannot make the transition to adult work and are cursed by maturity. Ryan had not only escaped that dead end, but he had also done it so effectively and quickly that he had gone from being praised by a Disney panel looking to hire Mouseketeers to being hailed by one of the top American film critics – all within a tidy decade. That U-turn alone was cause for triumph.

Despite positive reviews for *The Believer*, the film struggled to connect with audiences and went on to gross a total of only $416,925 worldwide. For Ryan, his work on the project was a tremendous success, with or without box-office validation: the film and its makers had provided him with an opportunity to radically and successfully reinvent himself.

As the summer came to an end, with his reputation growing fast, Ryan had his sights on a new film. Little did he know that this particular work would go on to become one of the most loved romantic movies of all time. Of course, who could imagine Ryan following his intense roles in *The Believer*, *The Slaughter Rule*, *Murder By Numbers* and *The United States Of Leland* with a part that would see him stepping into the guise of a romantic lead? This is what he did, though, and once more he was to take the least expected path and deliver a stunning performance in a film that would improbably transform him into a Hollywood sex symbol.

CHAPTER ELEVEN

A FORCE TO BE RECKONED WITH

L ate in the summer of 2002, Ryan packed up and headed down to South Carolina, where he was to be based until early 2003. He had signed up for a romantic drama called *The Notebook* and the film was to shoot on location in South Carolina.

It was to be directed by Nick Cassavetes, the son of actress Gena Rowlands (who was to appear in the movie) and one of Ryan's favourite filmmakers, John Cassavetes. Nick Cassavetes would be shooting from a screenplay co-written by Jeremy Leven and Jan Sardi. The duo had adapted the screenplay from the 1996 novel of the same name by the American novelist Nicholas Sparks, who has had other novels, before and since, such as *Message In A Bottle* and *Dear John*, adapted into films.

The project had been in casual development – without Nick

Cassavetes attached – since 1996, when New Line Cinema optioned the film rights to the novel before it was published. They saw a tremendous old-fashioned love story and immediately envisaged it translating into a powerful tearjerker of a film. After that initial excitement, what happened next was several years of New Line Cinema trying and failing to get the novel adapted into a screenplay that worked.

By the time they had a solid screenplay, Nick Cassavetes, who had also read the novel prior to its publication and loved it, was fresh from working on *She's So Lovely*, a film based on a script by his late father, co-starring Sean Penn and Robin Wright, and was ready to start work on *The Notebook*.

The screenplay told the story of a young couple, Noah (played by Ryan) and Allie (played by Canadian actress Rachel McAdams), who fall in love one summer, across a steep social divide, in the 1940s. Torn apart by Allie's wealthy family, who disapprove of her being with a young man from such a different social background, the storyline tracks the lovers' desperate attempts to end up united.

Throughout the film, the star-crossed lovers' story is narrated in the present day by an elderly man, Duke (played by James Garner), who reads a love story from his notebook to an elderly woman (Gena Rowlands), also a resident of the same care home for the elderly. As the story deepens, it becomes clear that the elderly woman has dementia and that she is Allie and the elderly man reading to her is Noah.

Ryan was surprised he landed the role as he had expected a classically handsome actor aka romantic lead to win the part. But he had been on Nick Cassavetes' mind as the perfect actor to play Noah. Cassavetes invited Ryan to come over to his home. When Ryan arrived, as he later relayed to *Company* magazine, Cassavetes immediately said to him, 'I want you to play this role because you're not like the other young actors out there in Hollywood. You're not handsome, you're not cool, you're just a regular guy who looks a bit nuts.'

Ryan told Cassavetes that, while he was flattered to be considered as a romantic lead, he didn't feel he was right for the part. He had never played a romantic part before and certainly not in a sweeping romantic epic like this. But Cassavetes was convinced that Ryan was perfect and, after much discussion, they compromised by agreeing to make a final decision once they had found an actress to play the part of Allie, since Ryan told Cassavetes he felt the film's success depended on who would be playing Allie.

In the end, it was Rachel McAdams who was cast as Allie. She was offered the part near the end of the audition process, in the same way that Ryan had been offered the part of Danny Balint right at the end of two rounds of auditions for *The Believer*. It was clearly meant to be.

McAdams, a fellow Canadian, saw the script for the first time a mere two days before doing the audition. She found that tight timeframe helpful, rather than pressuring, and arrived at the audition, as she put it, feeling 'full of the story'.

As per their discussions, Cassavetes had Ryan participate in the auditions for Allie, so they could measure chemistry. They had seen a lot of actresses quickly, who all tried out with Ryan. The recurring pattern that Cassavetes and Ryan noticed was that, after trying out a few scenes with Ryan, most of the actresses would ask if they were doing the part the way the director and actor wanted them to. That lack of conviction turned them off actress after actress; they wanted an actress to blow in who had a very clear idea how to play Allie.

She came in the guise of Rachel McAdams. She turned up and tried out for the scenes and, when asked if she had any questions, she said no, that she knew Allie and had a good grasp on what she was going to do. Ryan and Cassavetes were completely mesmerised by McAdams' confidence, as Ryan later told *About.com*: 'Rachel sort of came in at the end and she was the only one who when we asked if she had questions, said no. We said, "Do you know this girl?" She said, "Yeah." We said, "Do you want to talk about her?" And she said, "No. Let's just do it." We were like, "Whoa," and she wiped the tears off of her face and left. We said, "Okay, there's the movie. The movie is her."'

By a strange synchronicity of fate and destiny, it turned out Rachel McAdams was born in the same hospital as Ryan – St Joseph's in London, Ontario. She was born slightly earlier than Ryan, though: on 17 November 1978. But with her birthday just five days after his, it meant they were both Scorpio.

Her father, Lance, was a truck driver and her mother, Sandy, a nurse. Rachel was the eldest of three siblings. She also has a sister, Kayleen, and a brother, Daniel.

When she was seven, she started thinking about a career in show business, but that ambition didn't materialise until she turned 12 and attended a Disney camp. At the camp, she was steered towards a Shakespeare group who were putting on a production of *Macbeth* and she never looked back.

She went on to study for a BFA in Theatre at York University in Toronto and, during that time, landed herself a part in a TV pilot, *Shotgun Love Dolls*, and a Disney TV show called *The Famous Jett Jackson* (both 2001). With those lucky breaks came an agent and on she went, striding through half a dozen TV and film parts before landing a role on the Canadian TV comedy drama series *Slings And Arrows* (2003), playing the part of Kate McNab.

At the same time as her work on *Slings And Arrows*, she reached out to mainstream audiences with her role as Regina George in *Mean Girls*, acting opposite Lindsay Lohan, and then, of course, as Allie in *The Notebook*. By the time she won the part of Allie, she was twenty-three years old and Ryan was two years her junior.

By this stage, Ryan almost certainly would have had no idea that the film would catapult him into the big time, but he must at least have had a hunch that something was shifting since he had been offered a part that was very different from any other role that he had taken on thus far. He must have been thinking that, if he succeeded in pulling this off, it would be clear just how versatile an actor he was and he would be offered parts that had, until now, likely been off his radar. In short, once more, he had everything to play for.

To get in the mindset of Noah, Ryan moved down to South Carolina two months before the film officially started shooting. As previously, he would spend his days in character, this time taking an apprenticeship with a local cabinetmaker.

He became skilled at the craft and ended up making a series of chairs that appear in the movie and also a table from scratch – the very same table that Noah makes for Allie and then sets about making love to her on. Other days, he'd pass time by going out in a boat and rowing along the Ashley River.

The film was shot on location in South Carolina, in places such as Charleston, Mount Pleasant and Edisto Island, and then they filmed beach scenes in Los Angeles. Shooting began in late 2002, with a total estimated budget of $29 million. Cassavetes had decided to shoot the later period of the story first, which, of course, meant that Noah and Allie needed to look much older than they would in the earlier scenes.

To make himself look older, Ryan grew a beard and gained 20lb in weight, by eating more than usual and working out in such a way that he deliberately inflated himself with more bulk and muscle. Filming stopped for the Christmas holidays, during which time he needed to shed the weight he'd gained and reverse the bulky physique he had built up for himself. He also had to shave off his dense beard. When his reverse transformation was complete, the shoot could start again in January 2003.

The strange thing, given what would soon happen, was that Ryan and Rachel McAdams didn't exactly click during the shoot. Ryan later said of this to the *Guardian*, 'We inspired the worst in each other. It was a strange experience, making a love story and not getting along with your co-star in any way.'

The audience, of course, finds this hard to believe, given the crackling chemistry between the couple throughout the film. And, with hindsight, it seems hard to imagine that, behind the friction on set, Ryan and McAdams weren't somehow already falling for one another.

Ryan later all but admitted this to W magazine, saying, 'We were together long before we were physically together. All I knew is that she was a force to be reckoned with. How was I going to reckon with it, I had no idea.'

As it turned out, Ryan and McAdams would not get together during filming, nor indeed right afterwards. A certain amount of time would have to pass before they would wake up to how they felt about one another.

CHAPTER TWELVE

MOVING ON

As Ryan was busy shooting the second part of *The Notebook*, *The Slaughter Rule* opened at two cinema screens on 12 January 2003, taking just $1,461 on its opening weekend. The commercial performance of the film hardly picked up at all after that and it ended up grossing a total of $13,411 in the US.

This kind of box-office return was obviously completely at odds with the new film he was shooting, which everyone involved could already sense had the potential to become a major romantic blockbuster.

A week after *The Slaughter Rule* opened so quietly, *The United States Of Leland* premiered at the Sundance Film Festival on 18 January 2003. *Variety* published a lukewarm review, noting that Ryan's 'one-note, blankly disturbed act has none of the magnetic edge of his breakthrough work in *The*

Believer'. And this time around, the critic Roger Ebert wasn't on board, pronouncing the film a 'moral muddle'.

In short, *The United States Of Leland* was not a movie that was going to catapult Ryan's career to the next level, any more than *The Slaughter Rule* was. On 15 May 2003, though, the European premiere took place at the Cannes Film Festival and Ryan was still behind the film and believed in it.

Having finished work on *The Notebook*, he had no overt interest in signing up next to a large Hollywood film. As he became more experienced, he could see that the bigger the budget, the bigger the required payback. At this stage, he didn't want to appear in a movie, knowing that the way he acted was an essential component to its financiers recouping the budget and making a profit. He wanted to simply make great films – regardless of whether their budget was $1.5 million or $15 million – an artistic value that had been lodged in his mind when he was 14 and that video-shop employee had sent him home with a copy of David Lynch's *Blue Velvet*.

Midsummer, on 31 July 2003, *Contact Music* ran a news story under the heading 'Bullock and Gosling Split', which reported that: 'Hollywood actress Sandra Bullock has reportedly parted ways with her toyboy lover Ryan Gosling'. The article claimed that the couple had broken up several months earlier and that, while many might speculate that the split had happened because of their significant age difference, in fact, the reason was really a case of simple geography causing long-distance-relationship fatigue.

With Ryan based in Los Angeles and Bullock in Texas, the article implied the couple had struggled with the framework of a long-distance relationship and eventually called it quits. The news story said it was an amicable break-up and they would stay on good terms. As before, though, neither Ryan nor Bullock made a single public comment acknowledging that they had broken up, leaving the alleged relationship shrouded in mystery.

At this time, Ryan was settling into a new home: a loft apartment in Downtown Los Angeles. This part of the city was in the process of regeneration, led by high-profile building projects in the wake of the Frank Gehry-designed Walt Disney Concert Hall opening in 2003. It hasn't been reported where in Los Angeles Ryan was living before he moved into this home.

Despite the shift from the area being run down, it was still a not entirely obvious place for an up-and-coming actor to call home. But this was another way for Ryan to separate himself from the Los Angeles film industry. Instead of moving to a typical neighbourhood where he'd be constantly running into Hollywood folk, he elected to centre himself in a more real part of the city, one where he could play his Tom Waits albums at home and have them sound absolutely in sync with the neighbourhood. Ryan told the *Daily Telegraph* in 2007 that it was changing too quickly: 'When I first moved here there were tent cities on the streets and people were cooking on the corners, but now it's changing so fast. People used to think it was a dangerous place but I think it's more dangerous now that people with money are moving in.'

Late summer, Ryan was getting ready to start work on a new film called *Stay*. Shooting was scheduled to begin in

September. The film was to be directed by Marc Forster and had a budget of $50 million. Originally, it was to be directed by David Fincher, but he moved away from the project and into his place stepped Forster, who had previously directed films such as *Monster's Ball* and *Neverland*.

The film was written by David Benioff, who would later find acclaim as the screenwriter who adapted Khaled Hosseini's novel *The Kite Runner* for the big screen. *Stay* tells the story of a psychiatrist losing his grip on reality as he struggles to help a troubled patient.

The role of the psychiatrist Dr Sam Foster was played by Ewan McGregor, and Ryan plays Henry Letham, the young patient who challenges him by threatening to commit suicide shortly after their first meeting on the occasion of his 21st birthday. It seemed logical casting as Ryan had already excelled at playing an icy, detached, unreadable character in *The United States Of Leland* – and, for *Stay*, he would need to command a similar elliptical intensity for the audience.

In preparation for the shoot, Forster had Ryan and McGregor rehearse by learning each other's lines – and often had them say each other's lines just before they said their own lines in a scene. He wanted to drive home their interconnected and entwined roles and have the actors themselves feel slightly woozy about where one character ended and the other began. The shoot ended in January 2004.

Late in February 2004, Ryan found out that he had won the ShoWest Male Star of Tomorrow award. A month later, on 25 March, he attended the ShoWest Awards ceremony in Las Vegas to collect this accolade, wearing at this stage of his career what was a typically dressed-down outfit, consisting of a black shirt, blue jeans, a black blazer and worn black boots, and sporting stubble.

Meanwhile, *The United States Of Leland*, after touring a succession of European film festivals, opened in the US on limited release at 14 screens on 2 April 2004. Over its opening weekend, it grossed $48,384 and went on to take a total of $343,847 in the US.

The takings were nowhere near as low as *The Slaughter Rule*, but they were still weak. Added to the modest performance of *The Believer*, Ryan would have been associated with a trio of films that had failed to set the box office alight, had he not been connected to the commercial success of both *Remember The Titans* and *Murder By Numbers*.

When asked about the ShoWest award in interviews to promote *The United States Of Leland*, Ryan laughed it off, saying, as he saw it, nothing had changed. He told one reporter that, after they finished their interview, he would head out to get himself a cup of coffee and nobody would even bat an eyelid in the café and that was the genuine truth of his so-called emerging celebrity. Maybe it was true at that exact moment, but, in a matter of weeks, all that was going to change forever.

CHAPTER THIRTEEN

RED CARPETS
AND REALITY

The Notebook premiered at the Seattle International Film Festival on 20 May 2004. In anticipation of its premiere at the 5th Avenue Theatre, the festival billed *The Notebook* as 'an epic Hollywood romance'.

On the night of the screening, screenwriter Jeremy Leven introduced the movie to the audience. That night, the legend started that, by the end of the film, there was never a dry eye in the house – at almost every single screening, large proportions of the audience would end up sobbing uncontrollably during the closing scenes.

The official premiere took place in Los Angeles on 21 June. Ryan and all key cast and crew were present for the red carpet screening, staged at the Mann Village Theatre, in Westwood Village. Ryan wore a black suit, a tie worn undone and loose over a white shirt with the top button undone, and heavy stubble. He was very slowly starting to dress up for premieres.

In one photograph from the event, Ryan posed arm in arm with a smiling Rachel McAdams and they both look incredibly happy. From the photo, you'd conclude that they were already dating but, in an interview with *About.com* that McAdams did at the premiere, she was asked, 'Are you single now?' to which she replied, 'Yes, I am.'

McAdams wore a plunging, twenties-style, sleeveless vintage dress to the premiere, which had a cute story behind it – she was given the dress to wear when she did a photo shoot for *Elle* magazine and, afterwards, she was so smitten that she asked if she could buy it. The stylists happily sold her the dress, which had come from a vintage store in Los Angeles. When she was thinking about what to wear to the premiere, she thought straight away to wear that dress.

On 25 June, *The Notebook* went on general release and took $13,464,765 over its opening weekend. For a film with an estimated budget of $29 million, it was off to a great start at the world's box offices. It became a sleeper hit, fuelled by word-of-mouth buzz and went on to gross a massive $115,603,229 worldwide.

If Ryan's name had briefly been negatively associated with the lacklustre box-office performances of *The Slaughter Rule*, *The Believer* and *The United States Of Leland*, that was all over now. At this time, everyone was focused on how successful *The Notebook* was becoming and his reputation was inseparable from that snowballing success story.

With the film taking off, Ryan felt the intensity of mounting fame. He was still only 23 and had been working flat out since he won that *All New Mickey Mouse Club* show audition at the age of 12. Around this time, he felt like he needed to step out of the pressure cooker and consider life from a different perspective. He had made it now; his ambition to become a film actor was realised. With *The Notebook* causing audiences around the world to break down sobbing and box-office receipts stacking up feverishly, he was set for at least the next couple of films. From that place of suddenly realised success, he wanted to take time out to catch his breath and dial down the rush of adrenaline that was coming with his career taking off so rapidly.

How he took time out that summer has become something of a Hollywood legend: he later told GQ magazine that he took a job in a sandwich shop. As part of this role, he sometimes made sandwiches and sometimes stacked shelves. He has never said where the sandwich shop was, only that it was in Los Angeles, though a seasoned guess would be that the sandwich shop was in Downtown Los Angeles, close to his home. In a 2007 interview with the *Guardian*, the sandwich shop was described as a "local convenience store run by an Iranian" who became Ryan's friend, and Ryan said of the job of stacking shelves and making sandwiches, 'It was fun because I had a job where homeless people could tell me what to do.'

Those sceptical about this lovely story question how, in an age where every celebrity movement is tracked by social media, paparazzi, gossip columnists and bloggers, it was possible that no one spotted Ryan working away in this sandwich shop and snapped a picture on their cell phone or camera before uploading it to the internet or passed it on to a website or magazine. Or how it was possible that none of his colleagues gossiped to their friends and one of those friends couldn't resist posting something online.

The answer presumably is that Ryan was so discreet, so unlikely to be doing such a job, given that he had a hit film at the cinemas, that no one ever recognised him. Or, if they did, they didn't for a moment think it was Ryan Gosling, that it was merely a lookalike. After all, why on earth would an actor with a hit film out at cinemas be making sandwiches in a Los Angeles sandwich shop?

The reality is that Ryan doesn't follow formulas. Everything he does seems to be a reaction to what is expected next of him and working in a sandwich shop when he would be expected to be doing the rounds in Hollywood, auditioning for a romantic lead with a hefty pay cheque, is exactly how he likes to keep people – and most of all himself – guessing.

Of course, the deeper reality was more likely that to take a job like this, at a time like this, was the chess move of a person who caught wind of himself sailing off into the Tinseltown machine, with all its deadly glitter. Somehow, he instinctively knew that, to manage what was happening to him professionally, he urgently needed to get his feet pressed firmly back down on the ground. And the best way to do that was through hard work that left him with an aching back at the end of the day.

He would later try to rationalise what he was thinking, telling GQ magazine: 'I'd never had a real job,' before going on to criticise those who work in Hollywood, saying, 'They have meals. They go to Pilates. But it's not enough. So they do drugs. If everybody had a pile of rocks in their backyard and spent every day moving them from one side of the yard to the other, it would be a much happier place.'

Ryan has never said how long he worked at the sandwich shop that summer. But he did it for a while, so he could get his feet back on the ground. By November 2004, when he turned 24, with his life back in balance, he was ready to act again.

CHAPTER FOURTEEN

OFF-SCREEN
ROMANCE

In early 2005, Ryan met up with Rachel McAdams in New York and noticed there was suddenly a different chemistry between them. He told the *Guardian* that he didn't know what happened when they met this time, only that something had shifted: 'We started getting the idea that maybe we were wrong about each other.'

They quickly fell in love and what unfolded would turn into a two-year relationship. It was as if *The Notebook*, officially now considered the era's most romantic film, had spilled off-screen and wooed its co-stars into being bitten by the same vision that had wooed audiences from one end of the world to the other.

Rebuffing any connections with the film, Ryan would later tell *GQ* magazine that his and Rachel's story was totally different to that of Noah and Allie, and that, from his perspective, their coming together was far more romantic: 'I mean, God bless *The Notebook*. It introduced me to one of the great loves of my life. But people do Rachel and me a disservice by assuming we were anything like the people in that movie. Rachel and my love story is a hell of a lot more romantic than that.'

Ryan returned to acting in a gentle way. After the sandwich-shop stint, he was ready to act again but wanted to come back to the work slowly. This meant his first credit after *The Notebook* had blown up came in the form of his lending his voice to a documentary called *I'm Still Here: Real Diaries Of Young People Who Lived During The Holocaust*.

The film was directed by Lauren Lazin, written by Alexandra Zapruder and featured music by Moby. To give a voice to the diaries, various name actors and actresses were hired to read from them. *I'm Still Here* was adapted by Zapruder from her own 2002 book *Salvaged Pages: Young Writers' Diaries of the Holocaust*.

For his contribution, Ryan read from the diaries of Ilya Gerber, who was 17 years old when the Germans invaded his hometown of Kovno, Lithuania and herded the town's Jewish population into a ghetto. As deprivation, killings and deportations decimated Kovno's Jewish community, Gerber, whose family were protected by connections to high-ranking ghetto leadership, kept up his diary until the last-known entry on 23 January 1943. In the end, his fate is unknown but it is believed he perished in the ghetto.

Other diaries were read by the likes of Kate Hudson, Brittany Murphy, Amber Tamblyn and Elijah Wood. The film would eventually be donated as a gift to the US Holocaust Memorial Museum and Simon Wiesenthal Center for their permanent collection. But, before that, it premiered on MTV on 5 May 2005, to coincide with World Holocaust Day. In a review in *The New York Times*, the critic said of Ryan's contribution: 'Ryan Gosling reads the part of Ilya Gerber, an 18-year-old diarist in Lithuania, in a controlled and effective Rocky Balboa street accent.'

When the MTV Movie Awards ceremony came around on 4 June at the Shrine Auditorium in Los Angeles, Ryan and Rachel were present because *The Notebook* had been nominated for an MTV Movie award for Best Kiss. They were competing against Natalie Portman and Zach Braff for their kiss in *Garden State*, Gwyneth Paltrow and Jude Law (*Sky Captain And The World Of Tomorrow*), Jennifer Garner and Natassia Malthe (*Elektra*), and Elisha Cuthbert and Emile Hirsch for *The Girl Next Door*. Rachel had also been nominated for awards in the categories of Breakthrough Female and Best Female Performance.

When their kiss was announced as the winner of the Best Kiss award, Ryan and Rachel headed up to the stage and re-enacted the dramatic, full-blown *Notebook* kiss onstage, complete with Rachel leaping into Ryan's arms and wrapping her arms and legs about him. When they kissed – and this was a proper kiss, not two actors kissing – it was clear to the world that *The Notebook* had indeed been so romantic that its co-stars had fallen in love off-screen as well. For fans of the film, this affirmation that the pair had become a real-life couple couldn't have been any better.

The kiss was also a bold statement: they were a couple and it was official. It was a far cry from Ryan's reported relationship with Sandra Bullock, which had been shrouded in privacy, secrecy and mystery, and continued to be so.

On 14 August 2005, the *Teen Choice* Awards ceremony was held at the Gibson Amphitheatre in Los Angeles. For Ryan and *The Notebook*, it was a massive night. The ceremony made it clear just how much *The Notebook* had penetrated the teenage demographic and hooked them entirely with the film's love story.

That night, Ryan won the Choice Movie Actor: Drama award, triumphing over Samuel L. Jackson, Leonardo DiCaprio, Tom Cruise, Johnny Depp, Zach Braff, Joaquin Phoenix and Jamie Foxx.

Rachel McAdams won the Choice Best Actress: Drama award, beating her own similarly jaw-dropping list of formidable rivals: Kate Winslet, Natalie Portman, Scarlett Johansson, Brittany Murphy, Kerry Washington, Alexis Bledel and Amber Tamblyn.

Ryan was then once again onstage to collect another award – the Choice Movie Breakout Performance: Male. And a third time, with Rachel, to accept the Choice Movie Love Scene award. To top things off, the co-stars were also given the Choice Movie Chemistry award, the Choice Date Movie award and the Choice Movie: Liplock award. The eighth and final award of the ceremony saw *The Notebook* pick up the Choice Movie: Drama award.

Ryan attended this awards ceremony with Rachel, wearing scuffed Doctor Martens boots and a black suit and a T-shirt with 'Darfur' emblazoned across the front. He had his hair cut short in a crew-cut. Rachel was wearing a short black dress. In photographs taken at the ceremony, they look very much the couple madly in love, beaming at one another.

Winning a total of eight awards, he looked increasingly stunned as his name kept being called out as winner. And Rachel McAdams' eyes seemed to sparkle more brightly every time *The Notebook* picked up another award.

It seemed certain by the end of that awards ceremony that *The Notebook* had catapulted Ryan to a dizzying new level as an actor, and firmly announced him as a pin-up at the same time. From here on, he would be considered a sex symbol as much as he was regarded as a remarkably gifted actor. In this respect, *The Notebook* crossed him over into a mainstream realm, where he found his looks and ability under twin scrutiny. The fact that he was dating the co-star of the film that triggered all this of course only fanned the flames even higher. His relationship with Rachel was a gossip columnist's dream come true: the co-stars of one of the most romantic films of the era apparently don't get on while making the movie, but then, nearly two years later, they fall head over heels in love. It sounds like the absurd plot to a rather flimsy made-for-TV movie but it wasn't – this was really happening. Ryan and Rachel were now a couple in real life and happy for the whole world to know it.

CHAPTER FIFTEEN

HALF NELSON

The film that called Ryan properly back to acting was *Half Nelson*, although he couldn't possibly have known when he read the script and became very excited that, in choosing this small, intense, high-integrity project, he'd be setting himself on track for his first Academy Award nomination.

By the last page of the script, which told the story of Dan Dunne, a drug-using high school teacher who forms a redemptive relationship with one of his students, Ryan knew this was a role that would not only challenge him but would also blow the cobwebs off his sabbatical and counter head-on his new-found status as a romantic lead and Hollywood pin-up.

The fans who discovered his work with *The Notebook* must have been expecting him to play to formula and do what many actors have done when they have a hit film, which is to happily sign up for a clone project that seeks to capitalise on the success of its predecessor. It would have been the easiest thing in the world for Ryan to attach himself to another romantic drama and play the Noah card again. But he wasn't interested in going over ground already covered; he wanted to move ahead and keep himself – and the fans – guessing.

Half Nelson was co-written by Ryan K. Fleck and Anna Boden. The pair met when both were studying film at the Tisch School of the Arts in New York. Fleck has said that, when he was 12, he saw Spike Lee's *Do The Right Thing* (1989) and it moved him enormously and had a fundamental influence on him. That inner city, gritty influence was very much evident when he and his partner, Anna Boden, began conceiving and writing *Half Nelson*.

Originally, they wrote the film in 2001 but didn't know how to go about sending out or pitching their script because neither of them had an agent or any film industry credits under their belt yet. To try to build on the potential of what they were attempting to do, they bought a digital video camera and made a short film based on a digest version of their script, designed to demonstrate the feature film they had in mind and wanted to make. When casting the short film, they met Shareeka Epps while visiting performing arts schools and programmes within schools in the area and cast her as Audrey, aka Drey.

Epps was born in Brooklyn, New York, on 11 July 1989 and had graduated from a New York high school, so her perspective was completely authentic. Always passionate about singing and dance, she had performed in school productions of *West Side Story* and *Annie*. She was introduced to Roden and Fleck after her drama teacher recommended her to them, when they were dropping by schools in search of a student to cast as Drey.

To round off the small cast for the short film, Karen Chilton was asked to play Drey's mother and an actor called Matt Kerr was hired to play the teacher – then known as Mr Dunne. In the short film, the teacher's role is very minimal and bears no resemblance to the embellished role Dan Dunne would play in the feature-length version.

In the short film, Drey is 15 and lives with her mum and older brother. She becomes intrigued by one of her high school teachers, Mr Dunne, who is enigmatic and often turns his classes into intriguing philosophical questionings of life. One day, she stumbles upon him in the bathroom after a gym class, smoking crack. Her terror and shock and sense of betrayal that this could be happening give the film its intensity and edge.

Fleck and Boden managed to shoot their project for an estimated budget of $1,000. On completion, they gave it the title *Gowanus, Brooklyn*, and entered the film in the Sundance Film Festival. It was accepted for competition and screened in January 2004, when it won Boden and Fleck the Jury Prize – Short Filmmaking award.

The award led to an invitation for the pair to go back to Sundance and spend a week at the Writer's Lab, where they would receive advice and feedback on their feature-length script from a team of professional screenwriters. They jumped at the chance and found the week extremely useful.

Working with that kudos, they were able to sign up with an agent and begin work on adapting their original script into a full-length film. Since the short had focused on a high school student who finds out a secret about her teacher, the challenge now was to build a feature-length movie, which would also include more of the teacher's story.

The ensuing period between making the short film and casting the feature lasted almost two years. During that time, Epps and her family left Brooklyn and moved away to Upstate New York.

When they were finally in a position to make the film, the directors needed to track down Epps again, as there was no one who could play Drey as convincingly. They found her in Upstate New York and talked over how perfect she would be for the role again; Epps agreed to reprise her part and that answered one major casting question.

With regard to Dan Dunne, Boden and Fleck had it in their minds that they were searching for an actor who was likely to be in his mid-thirties. Apparently, Ryan came to read the script by chance – he hadn't been formally sent a copy, presumably because he would have seemed far too young for the part, being just 24 years old at this time. Once he had read the script and adored it, Ryan contacted Fleck and Boden and told them how much he was interested in both the part and the film they wanted to make. They explained that they were looking for an actor in his mid-thirties and Ryan said he understood that, but that he still wanted to meet them to talk about the film. They agreed and, as happened when Ryan turned up to audition for *The Believer*, their initial reservations based on age quickly melted away as he convinced them that, even though he was just 24, he knew he could play Dan Dunne.

They were also excited because his motivations were a far cry from many other actors they were considering – he wasn't particularly focused on the size of the pay cheque he'd be receiving for the role, he was merely interested in the part and the film.

With Epps and Ryan cast and a budget that is estimated to have been $1,000,000 in place, Fleck and Boden were finally ready to shoot their film (which by this time had been renamed *Half Nelson*) during July 2005. The scale of the budget meant they would need to shoot the entire film in just three weeks and, because many of the students in the classroom were real students and the school was available as a location only because it was summer vacation, everything would have to be set up to run effortlessly.

And more than that, although both had worked on documentaries before, Fleck and Boden's immediate challenge was to work with a full cast and crew – something that they weren't used to, having previously worked either with small crews or by doing everything themselves.

Meanwhile, Ryan was immersing himself in preparation for the part. A month before shooting began, he had moved to New York and was renting a small apartment in Fort Greene, Brooklyn. He had temporarily based himself there so he could spend several weeks shadowing the working days of a real-life 8th grade teacher, for research. Rachel McAdams, meanwhile, had recently finished shooting *The Family Stone*, alongside Claire Danes, Diane Keaton and

Sarah Jessica Parker, and was presumably able to spend time with Ryan in Brooklyn.

The teacher Ryan shadowed, David Easton, taught in an excited, inspiring way and Ryan found observing his class to be invaluable, just as he had found it crucial to sit in on Matthew Ryan Hoge's classes at the juvenile detention facility, as research for *The United States Of Leland*.

Observing the job of teaching at a high school allowed him to understand the nervousness a teacher feels every time he or she walks into a classroom, the strategies required to calm and motivate and discipline a class of students, the tactics involved in making a topic fascinating as opposed to pedestrian and, most pertinent to the film, the mentoring role performed by teachers, the integral trust bond between teacher and student, and the complicated teacher–student relationship, which has imposed and often hard-to-interpret boundaries. Ryan was able to get insights into all these crucial themes by shadowing David Easton.

In what was fast becoming his trademark style, Ryan's research was dedicated enough that his shadowing of Easton led to a close connection between the two men. So much so that, on one occasion, Ryan asked Boden to come and meet him at Easton's classroom. When she arrived, she peered through the door and mistook Easton for Ryan – it was uncanny how much he had learned from Easton. At this time, Boden and Fleck had still not cast the part of Dan Dunne's brother and, on seeing how close and similar Ryan and Easton had become, she cast David Easton.

Meanwhile, Fleck and Boden were keen to have Ryan and

Epps build up a rapport before shooting started and encouraged them to hang out as much as possible. One of their principal concerns was how well the two would connect because the entire film would hang on their chemistry, interaction and shared rhythm.

In an interview with *iofilm.co.uk*, Ryan Fleck talked about the chemistry between Ryan and the young girl who would play the student with whom his character connects: 'We could tell after the first scene that we did between Ryan and Shareeka, where she comes up to his car and calls him an asshole and he calls her a bitch. That played after its first take, everybody on the set was like, Whoaa. They knew that this was going to be alright, that these two had something cool going on.'

The many scenes in the movie with this intense connection between Ryan and Epps were built on how well the two got along off set. They developed a friendship, which everybody was aware of. Fleck spoke of how nice it was to witness this in the same interview with *iofilm.co.uk*: 'I think that his relationship with Shareeka, his friendship with her, was a very important basis for their characters' friendship in the film. They're still close, and by the time we started shooting they had really formed that friendship and maybe she had a little bit of a crush on him too.'

Beyond that, Fleck and Boden never saw any of the students who were appearing in the film act nervously around Ryan, which is credit to his humility, since they could easily have been intimidated or wowed by making a film with the star of *The Notebook* – especially since these students were all around 13 years old and Ryan and Rachel had just aced the MTV Movie Awards and blitzed the *Teen Choice* Awards that summer, too.

Fleck and Boden were enormously impressed by Ryan's ability to use physical expression and to use it as a constant texture. All the time, he was bowling out new ways to translate how his character was feeling with a glance or a hand gesture. Having earned his critical stripes with *The Believer* and his commercial stripes with *The Notebook*, Ryan went about making *Half Nelson* with an incredible, mesmerising power: it was as if his talent had been emboldened and deepened by his short sabbatical.

The shoot, as planned, wrapped after just 23 days and Ryan flew to Los Angeles. Soon after he arrived back home, Hurricane Katrina struck at the end of August and wreaked carnage across the Bahamas, the South of Florida, Mississippi, Louisiana, Cuba and Alabama.

Overwhelmed by the scenes of destruction on the news, Ryan felt he couldn't sit around without doing something to help. He packed up his car and drove down to Biloxi, Mississippi by himself, where he joined in with the clean-up effort. Once there, reports say that he helped rebuild a monastery badly damaged by the hurricane.

That Ryan would rush off to help with the clean-up process, especially after finishing an intense film shoot, is yet again evidence of his caring personality and sensitive nature – and also a marker of how grounded he was remaining, despite the overnight success *The Notebook* had brought him and, with it, the intense expectations for his future work.

That autumn, Ryan was busy promoting *Stay*, which had premiered at the Rio International Film Festival in Brazil on 24 September 2005. A month later, not helped by a string of tepid reviews, the film opened in US cinemas on 23 October 2005, taking $2,188,199 over the opening weekend. It went on to gross a total of $8,342,132 worldwide, which for a film with an estimated budget of $50 million was disappointing.

Even if Ryan might have felt a little glum over the way the film turned out – and, given that it hardly stands out in his filmography as one of his best, he likely did – he was distracted by the need to race against the clock to get a surprise new business venture ready in time for the doors to open.

CHAPTER SIXTEEN

PASTURES
NEW

F ew people knew that Ryan had spent much of 2005 working on a secret business venture. Around this time, he had provided the voiceover to the documentary *I'm Still Here: Real Diaries Of Young People Who Lived During The Holocaust*, prepared for and made *Half Nelson*, and still found time to drive South to help with the Hurricane Katrina clear-up. When 2006 began, though, word quickly spread about an entirely surprising venture in which he had invested heavily.

In January 2006, a new restaurant called Tagine opened its doors to diners in Beverly Hills, Los Angeles. Ryan's fans were surprised to learn that he was a co-owner of this petite, intimate new restaurant, along with a Moroccan chef and a sommelier, both of whom he had met while working at Water Grill, a restaurant on South Grand Avenue in Downtown Los Angeles, where he was living at this time.

Having a hand in opening a Moroccan restaurant was a way for him to further explore what had become a developing interest in Morocco and Moroccan culture. He hasn't explained why this came about, if he had visited Morocco and fallen in love with the place, its culture and its people. Or if it had come about via some other channel: for instance, through watching films or reading books about or set in Morocco.

The business partnership came about after Ryan was introduced to the cuisine of a Moroccan chef called Abdessamad 'Ben' Benameur via a mutual friend, a sommelier by the name of Christopher Angulo. One night Ryan asked Angulo to organise a party for a group of friends at Water Grill restaurant, and Angulo arranged for Benameur to cook a Moroccan-themed menu for the get-together.

Ryan was blown away by Benameur's cooking and struck up a rapport with the chef. The two got along, and Benameur invited the young actor to visit his home for a full-blown Moroccan feast. Ryan accepted the invitation and, over dinner, the two began talking about how hard it was to find an intimate restaurant in Los Angeles that offered impeccable Moroccan cuisine. Out of that conversation, they decided to open one themselves, in partnership with their sommelier friend, Christopher Angulo.

'He [Ryan] fell in love with my food,' Benameur told *Lifestyle* magazine. 'I invited him to my place and he decided to open a business with me.'

Ryan later explained to *Metro* his version of how he became a third of this partnership: 'At the time, I wasn't very busy, so I spent all my money on this restaurant. I spent a year working in it, now I love it and I think it's one of the best restaurants in L.A.'

The trio formally went into partnership in early 2005. It's probable that Ryan's interest in becoming involved in opening a restaurant had come about after his fabled stint at that sandwich shop. Perhaps this opportunity chimed with the fun he had making and serving food to customers.

Once the decision had been made by the three partners to open a restaurant, the first step was finding a suitable spot. They settled on a tiny location at 132 N. Robertson Boulevard in Beverly Hills. Previously, the premises had housed Mamounia, another petite Moroccan restaurant, which seemed like a smart business decision, since Los Angelenos who knew of Mamounia would already have this location marked in their minds as being a Moroccan restaurant.

Benameur has said that Ryan rolled up his shirtsleeves and became heavily involved in the renovation as they turned the former site of Mamounia into Tagine. Collectively, they set about furnishing the restaurant to their taste, fitting banquettes, lanterns, mirrors, in a bid to reference traditional Moroccan décor. They named the restaurant Tagine in honour of the earthenware dish in which classical couscous dishes are cooked, from one end of Morocco to the other.

Once the renovation and furnishing was complete, Tagine opened as a ten-table restaurant, offering diners an intimate, authentic Moroccan experience, as per the trio's business plan. This was achieved by fitting atmospheric lighting and furniture and by hanging photographs of Morocco on the walls, taken by a photojournalist friend of Ryan's called Dan

Winters. Ryan had met Winters in Georgia in 2001 and the two struck up a friendship, after discovering a mutual fondness for Linda Manz's performance in Terrence Malick's *Days Of Heaven*. 'You can't geek out with a lot of people about Linda Manz,' Gosling noted in *W* magazine. 'So we became best friends.'

The menu offered Moroccan specialities, such as bastilla, tagines, kefta and assorted couscous dishes. Today, it also offers Californian-themed additions for diners wanting diversity outside of a strictly traditional Moroccan restaurant, such as tiger shrimp, grand cru du potager and hummus. Tagine also offers a catering service for birthdays, weddings, bar mitzvahs, private parties and work events, helping the restaurant to expand its margin beyond the ten tables inside.

Ryan felt very connected to the restaurant when it opened and thought nothing of pitching in and waiting tables – which would stun diners when they realised their waiter was Hollywood's Ryan Gosling. Legend has it that he'd also jump in when there was a staff shortage. Benameur told *Lifestyle* magazine that Ryan is entirely unassuming when it comes to helping out at the restaurant and, when available, will take on any job that needs doing, 'One day, I was short on staff. He was in the kitchen; he jumped in as a dishwasher. He did the cooking classes with me.'

Central to the philosophy of the restaurant is Benameur wanting to recreate the fresh, delicious food he experienced as a child growing up in Morocco, when his mother would go to food markets and always have the freshest produce in her kitchen. Tagine offers two dishes that Ryan especially adores:

the first is the bastilla that Benameur makes as a starter; the second is a sea bass, which he serves with fresh chermoula sauce and assorted vegetables, variously sautéed, puréed and roasted.

Finally, when renovations, decorating and furnishing were complete, the restaurant was ready to open to diners in January 2006. By then, Ryan was ready to act again.

CHAPTER SEVENTEEN

FRACTURE

So the story goes, Ryan's cell phone rang and, when he answered it, he was inside a tent. Why he was in a tent, he has never disclosed. The caller was a film director, Gregory Hoblit, who wanted to talk to him about a movie he was intending to make: he had a part that he thought would be perfect for Ryan.

Later, this anecdote would become a big talking point in interview after interview, as Ryan admitted to one reporter after another that, yes, he did indeed take the call while in a tent, but, no, he would not elaborate on this story and explain why he was in a tent. Asked later by MTV if he was living in the tent, he replied, 'It's a really long story. But it's true. I spent a bit of time in a tent, and I read the script in there.'

The film Hoblit was calling about was *Fracture* and the part he was offering Ryan was that of an ambitious, restless

Los Angeles assistant district attorney by the name of Willy Beachum. To play Willy, Ryan would be acting opposite Anthony Hopkins – an actor he greatly admired – who would be playing Ted Crawford, an engineer who appears to have murdered his adulterous wife, Jennifer (played by Embeth Davidtz).

Though Crawford initially confesses to the police, he retracts his confession when the case first appears in court and so begins a game of cat and mouse between Beachum and Crawford, with Crawford constantly hinting that he might have murdered his wife, while Beachum, prosecuting for the district attorney's office, cannot produce any evidence to prove it.

Crucial to the tension is the fact that this is Willy's final case for the district attorney's office before leaving to take up a position at a private law firm, where he will be reporting to new boss and potential love interest Nikki Gardner (played by Rosamund Pike).

The screenplay was written by Daniel Pyne and Glenn Gers, based on a story by Pyne, who had previously written films such as *Pacific Heights*, *White Sands*, *Any Given Sunday* and *The Manchurian Candidate*.

Hoblit, who would be directing, came to the project with films such as *Primal Fear* and *Fallen* under his belt, as well as TV work as a director and producer on shows like *Hill Street Blues*, *L.A. Law* and *NYPD Blue*.

In preparation for the role, Ryan delved into the character he would play with his usual intensive research. He figured out an angle and constructed him as a man who was constantly eating, permanently wired on sugar. Ryan, who has a sweet tooth himself, said it was no great leap for him to craft a character who was always chewing jelly beans. *CanMag* quoted Ryan on the degree to which he used the detail of the jelly beans to develop Willy's character: 'It was one of those things where it was a guy that never slept obviously because he was working two jobs and couldn't really be sleeping, and so we just kind of made him this sugar-freak. He was always eating Jelly Bellies. Every day I would show up on set and I had a huge bag of Jelly Bellies and I'd try and make it through.' In the film, you see Willy chewing all the time and the intention is to make the audience feel that this is a man who is constantly salivating after his prey.

To round off his preparation, Ryan visited the law courts, where he would sit through trials and observe how the prosecution functioned and delivered. He also spent time with various lawyers who had worked on high-profile, very public cases, and he listened carefully and took notes as they explained their methodology and process to him.

Ryan said later that he got right inside the psychology of Willy Beachum by profiling him as being fundamentally motivated by a wild sense of ambition and, as a result, decidedly more corrupt than the usual, renegade 'good guy' on the right side of the law, who tends to populate films of this genre.

He found it interesting, as he told *About.com*, that Willy viewed the rules and procedures of the law to be effectively inconvenient to his own agenda: 'In the whole film doing the right thing is kind of a pain in the ass for him and he never makes some kind of huge moral shift.'

In the middle of his research, *Half Nelson* premiered at the Sundance Film Festival on 23 January 2006. The film was the first one to feature Ryan since *The Notebook* had been released and went on to become such a massive success. As a result, Fleck and Boden wanted to manage this well, since *Half Nelson* was a very different kind of movie. They were understandably nervous that the critics who loved Ryan in *The Notebook* would have a tough time now accepting him as a drug-abusing high school teacher. The switch from wholesome romantic lead to gritty character study was a transition that made sense to Ryan and everybody involved with *Half Nelson* and at Sundance, but there was a genuine fear that a lot of negativity could be directed at *Half Nelson* because it did not present Ryan as fulfilling the wishes and desires of those who could not separate him in their minds from how he had played Noah in *The Notebook*.

To counter this, in the run-up to the premiere at the Sundance Film Festival, there was a gentle publicity drive that emphasised the way the movie had been made, its use of non-actors and the lovely on- and off-screen friendship between Shareeka Epps and Ryan. And the drug theme of the film was played down, so it wouldn't be jumped on and taken out of context as a sensationalistic aspect.

The fears proved unfounded and the film was extremely well received when it premiered at Sundance and, in the days after, the producers received several offers from distributors. In the end, between offers from Miramax and ThinkFilm, the producers went with ThinkFilm, who had pledged to make sure the film opened at cinemas in at least 15 different cities across the US.

The movie was small in scale and very much framed as an independent effort. This was another way that Ryan bought himself some breathing space after the epic trajectory that he underwent as a result of his performance in, and association with, *The Notebook*. But *Half Nelson* was such a mesmerising work and Ryan's performance so confident, so assured, so completely believable, that the movie would go on to bring him an ever greater degree of attention.

Meanwhile, with a budget of $10 million, *Fracture* began shooting in Los Angeles in February 2006. For Ryan, it was exhilarating to act opposite Anthony Hopkins and they sparked effectively together so that the scenes between them are often reminiscent of those between Jodie Foster and Hopkins in *The Silence Of The Lambs*. As in the earlier film, Hopkins seems to savour every second of playing Ted Crawford as a glacial, brilliant man who sees it as a delicious game of chess to manipulate and play with Willy's ego.

Ryan has said that his biggest challenge in making the film was staying in character in scenes with Hopkins. As Ryan Gosling, he would be in awe of Hopkins' acting and would get a constant thrill from watching how he played each scene. But, as Willy Beachum, he had to express frustration, irritation and impatience when interacting with Ted Crawford. He told *About.com* that he found it really hard to switch off his real-life appreciation of each moment with Hopkins and, instead, override it with his character's place in each scene: 'I'm enjoying everything he's doing so much that I'm trying to get over the fact that I'm in scenes with Anthony Hopkins. And every time he does something I'm like [stares out wide-eyed]. I just want to watch him and I have to remember that I'm in a scene, too, and I have to play the character and be serious. My character doesn't enjoy him at all and it was really tricky to enjoy him as much as I was and try and pretend like I'm not.'

Ryan was also struck by Hopkins' on-set behaviour. He has admitted that he was blown away by how constantly creative Hopkins was – how they'd have a short break and Hopkins would go off to his trailer and work on a painting. Or they'd stop for a few minutes and Hopkins would make a doodle – and, from where Ryan was standing, it would be a great doodle. 'He's constantly moving,' Ryan told *About.com*. 'He's so inspiring to watch. He's either painting or he's writing or he's directing or he's composing. He never stops.'

He also appreciated how much fun his fellow actor was to work with and, in one interview, spoke lovingly of how Hopkins had entertained cast and crew with wildly authentic dog barking – which Ryan, as a dog owner himself, said was so true to life that he could almost detect the breed of dog Hopkins was impersonating.

For Ryan, the shoot was an incredible experience. He was given the chance to work with an actor whom he considers to be a 'master' and, through this, he learned a lot, absorbing Hopkins' method of acting and how he went about conducting himself while making a film. The movie also built ever further on Ryan's inching towards Hollywood. It didn't announce his outright embrace of bigger-budget films, but, following on from *Murder By Numbers*, *The Notebook* and *Stay*, it showed that he was starting to feel comfortable alternating mainstream roles with more personal, independent film roles.

Meanwhile, *Half Nelson* opened at US cinemas on 11 August 2006 – initially at just two screens in New York, where the film took $53,983 over its opening weekend. That same weekend, on the TV show *Ebert And Roeper*, Richard Roeper and special guest critic Kevin Smith, director of independent films such as *Clerks*, *Mallrats* and *Chasing Amy*, who was standing in for Roger Ebert, reviewed the movie on the show and said it was one of the ten best films he had seen over the past decade. Powered by this, the film then opened at cinemas in Los Angeles and other cities and, encouraged by positive reviews, went on to take $4,660,481 worldwide, opening it up into a commercial success.

CHAPTER EIGHTEEN

BIANCA

A fter *Half Nelson*, Ryan didn't swing back to signing up for another film like *The Notebook*. Instead, he tunnelled deeper into independent film, attaching himself to a movie that gave him the opportunity to once more play a complex, unusual character. In fact, the role he signed up for would be the most offbeat he had ever played or has ever played since. As ever, his strategy was to keep himself challenged and his fans and critics guessing.

The film was called *Lars And The Real Girl*. It was written by Nancy Oliver, who had previously written extensively for the dark, yet popular TV series *Six Feet Under*. Her script told the story of a young man, Lars Lindstrom, who lives with his brother, Gus, played by Paul Schneider, and his brother's pregnant wife, Karin (Emily Mortimer), in a small town in Wisconsin.

Lars and Gus had lost their mother when she was giving birth to Lars, a trauma that seems to have defined Lars, and, at the time the film's story opens, the brothers have just lost their father, too. During this time of grief, Lars (who lives in a converted garage behind the family home) hears colleagues at work talking about a blow-up sex doll you can order from the internet. Following their conversation, he orders one of these dolls. When it arrives, he treats it as if it's a real girlfriend and names it Bianca.

Thereafter, Lars behaves as if he's met a real woman and fallen in love with her and he couldn't be any happier. He introduces Bianca into every aspect of his life. When he takes her out with him, the inhabitants of the small town think he's having a breakdown.

It's the kind of role to which Dennis Hopper would also gravitate. One thinks of a film like *River's Edge*, in which Hopper's character also had a relationship with a blow-up doll and talked to her too. While *Lars And The Real Girl* sounds as if it will be sinister in the way that Hopper's engagement with the blow-up doll in *River's Edge* was, it's not – it's more of an offbeat, whimsical film. It's exactly the kind of independent American movie in which one expects to see the actress Patricia Clarkson, who, fittingly, does indeed appear in the film, playing the character Dagmar.

The film was directed by Craig Gillespie, an Australian filmmaker whose directorial debut *Mr Woodcock*, starring Billy Bob Thornton, ended up being released at almost the same time as *Lars And The Real Girl*. Gillespie told *Filmmaker* magazine that, as soon as he read Nancy Oliver's script, he knew that not only did he want to make the film, but also exactly how he wanted to make it: 'It's the only script I've read that I knew exactly how I wanted to shoot. I don't know particularly why that is, but there's a style to her writing that I completely got the tone of what was going on, and that hasn't happened before or since.'

On a budget of approximately $12 million, the shoot lasted 31 days. They filmed on location in Ontario, Canada, which for Ryan meant heading home. Prior to that, the film had been a long time in the making. Gillespie said that, from the moment he was excited about the script, it took a year to get the movie into production and that he had also been preparing with Ryan for several months before shooting began.

It was key to the film's success that Ryan was completely ready to play the part because the movie is essentially a character portrait and, because of that, the way Ryan played Lars would either lift it up or not.

The director told Ryan that he had in mind a film that would evoke many 1970s films, in particular several made by Hal Ashby. A prime example, in terms of a template for the kind of film Gillespie wanted to make, was Ashby's 1979 movie *Being There* – an offbeat classic starring Peter Sellers. Another Ashby film referenced often was the offbeat, mordantly humorous *Harold And Maude*, which came out in 1971.

Before all this, Gillespie, once on board to direct the film, immediately thought of meeting with Ryan to see if he'd be right to play Lars. Gillespie told *Filmmaker* magazine that he knew within 45 minutes of sitting down with the actor that he'd be perfect for the part: 'He has this accessibility and this openness about him, and as we discussed the scenes I could see this innocence in the way that he would think about things.'

To prepare for the role, Ryan immersed himself in what Lars would be like. He began to build a character, giving him a moustache, also a blanket that he was attached to, and decided that he would need to gain weight in order to capture the sense that this character existed beneath layers of comforting padding.

He also felt that, if Lars is the type of person who mostly sits around in his converted garage home, then he'd carry the extra pounds of someone beached on a sofa. With his own lean physique, it wouldn't feel true onscreen: that was Ryan's rationale for setting about gaining weight.

This commitment to character once more made those around him presume that he was following a strategy of Method acting, leading to a funny story about this on the *Lars And The Real Girl* shoot.

Ryan said that, during the first week's work on the film, the driver assigned to ferry him about didn't speak to him at all. Ryan explained to *indielondon* that he felt the need to address this: 'Finally, I said: "I've been talking to you all week and you never say anything back. It's not nice." And he said: "I was told not to talk to you. I heard you were real "method" and I was only supposed to call you Lars and not supposed to look you in the eye!" I was so embarrassed.'

To film 196 scenes in 31 days meant there were days on the shoot when Ryan would be playing Lars at different points in the film – which, aside from costume changes taking place multiple times in one day and make up, too, meant that he had to constantly be on his toes and capable of stepping into Lars' head at many different points in his journey during the film, at different times of each day. To be able to handle this was a sure sign that Ryan was becoming an increasingly experienced and adaptable actor.

At all times, the blow-up doll – Bianca – was treated as if she was an actress working on the film. Ryan said in an interview with *Beliefnet* that, at one point, he asked Gillespie how they were going to work with Bianca on the set and Gillespie replied, 'I'm going to treat her as though she has a nudity clause in her contract.' It was this commitment to making the story credible that led to a scenario that so easily wins over the audience and steers them away from watching the film and thinking it's absurd and too weird to connect with.

Ryan has said that, in practical terms, it meant, between takes, a crew member would do things like hand Bianca a magazine to read. He has also said that they took it so seriously that Bianca would actually undergo costume changes in what was known as her trailer. At all times, they felt it was fundamental to the credibility of the work they were doing that the cast and crew bought into Bianca being Lars' real-life girlfriend, as Ryan told *About.com*: 'The girls that were taking care of her would give her magazines in between takes. She was always treated like one of the actors. And everybody on the crew went out of their way to respect Lars' idea of her.'

Ryan later told *Entertainment Weekly* that it became so the blow-up doll was his co-star in the film: 'You would have moments where you thought she looked at you, or said something to you or moved.'

He has said that in time even the most sceptical cast and crew members were slowly won over by the idea that Bianca was real. At first a lot of people thought it was ridiculous that Bianca was being treated as a real actress, but then, as the days passed, Ryan said he'd notice small shifts, like a crew member sitting and having a cup of coffee with her as if she were a real person.

While Gillespie had those Hal Ashby films in mind, Ryan had a private film playing in the back of his mind too, which he called on to make sure he worked in this film exactly as he wanted to. The film was Claude LeLouch's 1966 film *A Man And A Woman*, starring Jean-Louis Trintignant and Anouk Aimée as a widow and widower who come together and fall in love.

Ryan said in an interview that this is one of his favourite all-time films and that he'd always loved a remark by LeLouch about how one must always have a cold setting for a love story, as the story needs to warm up as its characters fall in love. When playing Lars, he was mentally referencing back to this French film for inspiration and to keep himself on the right track.

Once the shoot ended, it seemed natural to Ryan that he should take Bianca home with him and, during interviews later, at the time of the film's release, he often spoke of how Bianca had stayed in his life and lived with him at his home in Los Angeles. He joked with *indielondon* about how he found it hard to stop treating her like a real person: 'She's at my house right now – reading a book by the window. I have a Bianca, and Craig [Gillespie] has a Bianca. When they dropped her off at my house I was going out. I thought: "I can't really leave her." So I brought her out to the bar. As soon as you bring Bianca the whole party livens up!'

As Ryan recuperated after making a film as intense as *Lars And The Real Girl*, he heard the first rumours that there was a possibility that he might receive an Academy Award nomination for his work in *Half Nelson*. Having just turned 26, was he really on the brink of that scale of recognition for his acting ability? ThinkFilm, the distributor of *Half Nelson*, seemed to think there was a real chance of his making the list of nominees. Everybody connected to Ryan knew that, if he did get nominated, it would give the film a huge boost and simultaneously catapult his career into orbit.

CHAPTER NINETEEN

ACCOLADES & AFRICA

Nominations for the 79th Academy Awards were announced on 23 January 2007 and this proved a career milestone moment for Ryan. As everyone connected to *Half Nelson* had hoped, his name had indeed made this most prestigious of all Hollywood award lists. He had been nominated, as anticipated, in the category of Best Performance by an Actor in a Leading Role.

The nomination was a massive moment for the film, since it offered a small movie such as this an overnight volume of attention and publicity that the producers could never have afforded or even dreamed of. Its gentle takings at the box office would be swiftly levelled by critical recognition given to the film from this most exalted level.

The nomination set *Half Nelson* among a flock of movies with colossal budgets and immaculately slick marketing and publicity machines. Ryan's nomination was a triumph for all those connected with the project who worked so hard to realise a story whose gritty integrity fell far outside typical Hollywood channels of storytelling.

Overnight, all the expectation that Ryan might receive a nomination exploded and the media ran with what had suddenly turned into an underdog story: a lovely story of a little film shaming all the big-budget films.

As the ceremony drew ever closer, the hype surrounding Ryan's nomination grew louder. In a news story about his nomination, shown on *ABC News*, the reporter visited Ryan near his then home in Downtown Los Angeles. As they walked about the streets, camera in tow, Ryan laughed off the idea that *The Notebook* had turned him into a Hollywood heartthrob. He seemed uncomfortable with the idea that he was seen by anyone as a heartthrob, dreamboat or pin-up actor – it likely reminded him too much of his early career, the TV work, and he didn't want to be treated as some kind of pop star.

He had walked away quite consciously from that route early on after playing a Mouseketeer – he had no interest in becoming the kind of entertainer or actor whose poster would end up tacked to the wall of a teenage girl's bedroom. Of course, he was aware that, after *The Notebook*, this was probably now happening. He wasn't against it, but it wasn't something he was personally comfortable with. It didn't fit with his values of integrity, those set by David Lynch's *Blue Velvet* and the albums of Tom Waits when he was just 14 years old. He was all about the work and he wanted that celebrated, not the way he looked.

In the same *ABC News* feature, he also dismissed the idea that he only took on dark, despairing roles – a Jewish Nazi, troubled teenagers who kill, a suicidal young man, a drug-addicted teacher – saying that he gravitated to these parts because such films represented reality as he understood it. He said that he was sent many scripts but looked through most of them getting no real sense of a beating heart. He explained that the roles he takes on were those of people he feels connected to, whose stories offer him a chance to address something from his own life, from inside his own psyche. He doesn't see them as marginalised, more as under-represented in typical Hollywood fare: 'It has nothing to do with the dark side or being attracted to that or anything. It's more about a lot of Hollywood's idea of reality doesn't really have anything to do with my reality.'

The interview concluded with Ryan talking about a trip he had recently made to Africa and a film he hoped to direct about child soldiers involved in conflict in the north of Uganda. He said he was very committed to making the film and, with it, drawing attention to the plight of children forced into the conflict serving as soldiers.

The idea for the film harked back to 2005, when Ryan visited Chad to shoot a documentary about Darfur refugee camps. The scenes he saw there and the people he met left an indelible mark on him. It was on this trip that he first learned about children who are forced to become soldiers. He said he was appalled by the idea that children were kidnapped from their homes and forced to become soldiers, as well as by the scale of killing in that region: 'My hope is that you put people in the shoes of these kids, so that you have to go through it with them.'

His interest was strictly personal – he made a point of saying in interviews that he wasn't serving the interests of a charity or NGO. Presumably, he was also mindful not to seem like just another actor or actress who, on achieving a certain level of fame, adopts a barrage of charitable causes as if they feel the need to 'give back' some of the fame, wealth and privilege they have come into. It wasn't about that; this was about Ryan trying to help these children in drawing attention to their plight.

This was the first time that Ryan was suddenly talking about social affairs and global politics. It was also showing another dimension to what appeared to be a strong connection to Africa, its people and their cultures. First, he had expressed his interest in Morocco and North Africa with the opening of Tagine. Now he was talking about having personally headed out to conflict-stricken parts of Africa to see what was happening with his own eyes. And, out of that, he felt a need to write a screenplay about what was happening in the north of Uganda.

It was a sign of his ongoing restlessness and ambition that he was already looking at ways to go beyond acting and turn his attentions to writing and, with that, the possibility of directing his own film.

The *ABC News* report ended with Ryan saying that, when he was growing up and going through difficult patches, his mother never once stopped loving him, and stood by him despite his challenging behaviour. He intended to take her with him to the Academy Awards ceremony for, without her love and support, none of the acclaim he had come to receive would ever have happened: 'She deserves to kind of go to a fancy party and put on a fancy dress, have a bunch of fancy people tell her she did a good job. Because she did. Because I'd be scalping tickets for this show if it wasn't for her.'

Outbursts such as this further endeared him to the fans who had come on board to his talents with *The Notebook*. They loved his gentlemanly devotion to the women in his life – his mother, his sister and, of course, Rachel.

The 79th Academy Awards ceremony was staged at the Kodak Theatre in Los Angeles on 25 February 2007 and hosted by Ellen DeGeneres. Ryan was in attendance – with his mother as promised. The nominations for the Academy Award Best Actor in a Leading Role were read out by Reese Witherspoon. Ryan was up against Leonardo DiCaprio (*Blood Diamond*), Peter O'Toole (*Venus*), Will Smith (*The Pursuit Of Happiness*) and Forest Whittaker (*The Last King Of Scotland*).

After the clip from *Half Nelson*, the camera zoomed in on a stubbly Ryan sitting beside Donna. He had his arms crossed and, in a sign of how seriously he was taking this, he was wearing a tuxedo – gone were the dusty combat boots, the faded black jeans, the casual T-shirt. As Forest Whittaker was announced as the winner and headed up to the stage, the camera sought out Ryan and showed him giving Whittaker a standing ovation and grinning, then sitting back down as his fellow actor began to make his acceptance speech.

In the aftermath of the Oscar buzz, Ryan was even keener

to try to find backing for his script about the child soldiers in Uganda. It now had a title: *The Lord's Resistance*. He had been developing the screenplay with a friend called Noaz Deshe and focusing the story on the lives of children forced to become child soldiers by Joseph Kony, the leader of the Lord's Resistance Army.

As Ryan told *Entertainment Weekly*, 'He [Kony] cut off their lips and their ears, and their noses and their breasts. And he turned little girls into sex slaves. I want to tell a story about them, with them, starring them.'

As a project, it was quickly developed enough that, on 1 February, a news story appeared in *Variety* magazine about the film, under the headline 'Gosling recruits "Army" for directorial debut'. The article stated that Ryan was to direct the feature with a cast of non-professional actors and real-life child soldiers, recruited in East Africa. It also revealed that he was close to getting financing in place and saw his directorial debut as a priority over the many offers of roles that had come flooding in since he had received his *Half Nelson* Academy Award nomination.

Celebrations continued when, on 24 February, Ryan won the Best Male Lead award for his performance in *Half Nelson* at the 22nd Independent Spirit Awards. Shareeka Epps was also a winner that day, taking the Best Female Lead. The movie had also gathered nominations for Best Director and Best Feature.

It seemed the film couldn't stop collecting award nominations. *Half Nelson* also won the 2007 AFI Film of the Year award, and at the 2006 Deauville Film Festival Ryan

Fleck was awarded the Special Jury Prize and the Revelations Prize. Ryan was given second place in the BSFC Best Actor award at the 2006 Boston Society of Film Critics Awards and was nominated for the Critics Choice Award at the 2006 Broadcast Film Critics Association Awards. And that wasn't the full extent of the nominations. Ryan would also collect nominations for Best Actor award at the 2006 Chicago Film Critics Association Awards, Best Actor at the 2007 Chlotrudis Awards, Best Actor at the 2006 Dallas-Fort Worth Film Critics Association Awards, Best Actor in a Motion Picture: Drama at the 2006 Satellite Awards, Outstanding Performance by a Male Actor in a Leading Role at the 2007 Screen Actors' Guild Awards, Best Performance, Male at the 2006 Toronto Film Critics Association Awards and Best Actor at the 2007 Vancouver Film Critics Circle Awards.

He also won the Best Actor prize at the 2007 Las Palmas Film Festival, the NBR Breakthrough Performance: Male award at the 2006 National Board of Review Awards; third place in the NSFC Best Actor award at the 2007 National Society of Film Critics Awards, second place in the NYFCC Best Actor award at the 2006 New York Film Critics Circle Awards and the Best Actor award at the 2006 Stockholm Film festival.

If that list left you reeling, spare a thought for how Ryan must have felt after that one single performance brought him such widespread critical acclaim. What is interesting is that *Half Nelson* had brought him the polar opposite kind of praise to *The Notebook*. It had earned him the respect of almost the entire film critic community and the respect of the programmers and staff of the world's many discerning film festivals. If *The Notebook* spoke to mainstream cinema audiences, *Half Nelson* was for film buffs, film fanatics and film industry people. It was as if he had gone out into another constituency with this film and won a landslide victory.

With the two films, Ryan had been able to achieve the improbable outcome of one actor appealing equally to two entirely different audiences and demographics. It would show to the film industry that he was entirely versatile and that he could turn his hand to any kind of role, bringing the same onscreen charisma to it.

On 1 March, an opinion piece co-authored by Ryan with John Prendergast, co-founder of the Enough Project, was published on the ABC news website under the headline 'At War In The Fields Of The Lord'. The piece reflected on what the pair had witnessed on a trip to Uganda in February 2007. On theme with Ryan's screenplay in progress, the piece opened by talking about how a young man had been rehabilitated and was now studying and living a life far removed from the days when he was forced to become a child soldier.

In the background of Ryan and Prendergast's piece loomed Joseph Kony and the Lord's Resistance Army. As part of this awareness campaign, the writers also discussed the conflict in Uganda on the ABC programme *Be Seen, Be Heard*, which aired in March 2007.

This season of nominations, awards, award ceremonies and talking about Africa was punctuated by Ryan stepping out onto another red carpet on 11 April 2007, for the premiere of *Fracture* at the Mann Village Theatre in Westwood, Los

Angeles. Ryan turned up to the event with his sister Mandi, wearing a white shirt and a grey Lacoste cardigan under a black blazer. He posed grinning for the cameras, with his arm around Mandi, who was wearing a glamorous blue dress.

A day later, the film also screened at the Phoenix Film Festival before going on general release on 22 April. It took $11,014,657 million over the opening weekend, encouraged by mostly positive reviews, and went on to gross a healthy $91,354,215 worldwide. Critically and commercially, Ryan was on a roll.

CHAPTER TWENTY

AWARDS, ICE CREAM & ENDINGS

In June 2007, with so many offers to choose from, *Variety* reported that Ryan had signed up for a film that would be an adaptation of Alice Sebold's bestselling novel *The Lovely Bones*.

Published to widespread acclaim in 2002, the book told the story of the rape and murder of a young girl, called Susie Salmon. The girl's story is narrated from the afterlife and thematically followed Sebold's 1999 memoir *Lucky*, which chronicled the brutal rape attack she herself suffered as a teenager. Ryan loved the novel, as he'd mentioned at a press junket for *Lars And The Real Girl*, saying of Sebold's book, 'I read that book a long time ago. I think it's so beautiful, and it's a totally unique story. I'm trying to think, there is nothing really like it.'

The screenplay was written by Fran Walsh and Philippa

157

Boyens, in collaboration with the film's director, Peter Jackson. This writer/director team of three was the same trio who had made the wildly successful *Lord Of The Rings* series.

Ryan was cast in the role of Jack Salmon, the father of Susie, the girl who is raped and murdered. Rachel Weisz was cast as Jack's wife, Abigail Salmon.

When Ryan learned he had got the part, he admitted that he felt a little nervous about how, as a 26-year-old, he was going to play the older father and do so convincingly, but everyone involved with casting him told him that he was right for the role and it would work.

The film, which had a $65 million budget, was due to start shooting later in October, on location in Pennsylvania and New Zealand. Prior to that, with his usual dedication to research and character development, Ryan had come to the conclusion that, to convey the necessary maturity for the part, he would need to gain a significant amount of weight and grow a beard. In a way, he was looking back to what had worked for *The Notebook*, when he needed to shoot those later scenes and give credibility to Noah's ageing.

The beard took care of itself. But, to gain the weight, he needed to stop exercising and, aside from eating more than usual, he began melting down tubs of Häagen-Dazs ice cream and drinking the liquid whenever he was thirsty under the hot Los Angeles summer sun. It proved a quick way to gain weight and, by the time the movie was about to start shooting, he had gained a hefty 50lb.

During that preparation season, *Lars And The Real Girl* premiered on 2 October 2007 at the Academy of Motion

Picture Arts and Sciences in Beverly Hills, Los Angeles. Ryan was in attendance, sporting the thick beard he was growing for *The Lovely Bones*. Ever smarter at premieres and awards ceremonies, he was wearing a crisp, white shirt and a grey smoking jacket with a rose in the buttonhole. *Lars And The Real Girl* opened at cinemas on 14 October 2007 and, despite positive reviews, grossed just $90,418 at the box office across its opening weekend. Although it would go on to take $11,293,663 worldwide, against an estimated budget of $12 million, the film proved too idiosyncratic and particular to make a connection with a broader audience. Everyone knew that this film was particular and was never going to speak to Ryan's *Notebook* fan club.

A week later, giving interviews to promote the film's release, Ryan talked excitedly about *The Lovely Bones*, mentioning how much he was looking forward to working with Peter Jackson on the adaptation: 'He's fearless as a director. He takes on things that you kind of have to be crazy to take on. To do *Lord Of The Rings* you have to kind of be nuts because there is no way you are going to win. You are always going to have naysayers and people saying you ruined it or whatever. But he's my kind of nuts because he doesn't care and he does it anyway.'

Then, on 21 October, *About.com* reported the shock news that Ryan had left *The Lovely Bones* project, mere days before shooting was about to begin. The report explained that he had apparently turned up bearded and 50lb heavier, as he intended, and that his appearance had completely stunned the producers. It turned out that the way he was envisaging playing Jack Salmon was not how the makers of the film had envisaged this. When they hired him, he had weighed in at 150lb and now, here he was, weighing in at over 200lb.

The producers said he needed to lose the weight, get in shape and that, via make-up and all kinds of tricks, they would be able to give him the appearance of an older man. Despite this compromise, Ryan wasn't feeling the change in direction and, after further discussions, decided it was best if he left the project. He was replaced by Mark Wahlberg.

Ryan was hugely disappointed as he later told *ABC*: 'I just showed up on set, and I had gotten it wrong. I really believed in it. I was excited about it. I showed up, and they said, "You look terrible." And I said, "I know! Isn't it great?" "No, it's not. Go hit the treadmill." Then I was fat and unemployed.'

Suddenly off the project, Ryan let creative differences be exactly that and, putting the integrity of his work first, stepped aside in a very professional manner. Of course, leaving such a high-profile film at the last minute was a gamble and, in doing so, he was rolling the dice on his career being safe in the aftermath.

Ryan would later look back on this bump in the road and explain to the *Guardian* that he neither quit nor was he fired: 'It was mutual. I mean, it wasn't dramatic – it just became clear that it would be better with someone else. I feel like it's a better movie with Mark Wahlberg in it. You have to know what you can't do, too.'

Despite this momentary wrong-footing, Ryan's star was ever rising, with or without *The Lovely Bones*. When the November 2007 issue of *GQ* magazine hit newsstands, Ryan was on the cover. To the surprise of his fans and to the dismay of *The Notebook*'s many fans, in the interview he said that he and Rachel McAdams were no longer an item. It was only a single comment on the relationship having ended but, given how little he says of his love life, it carried tremendous impact: 'The only thing I remember is we both went down swingin' and we called it a draw.'

It seemed as if he was in the thick of an era of endings. First, *The Lovely Bones* project had come to an abrupt end. And now, he and Rachel were over too and fans were left in the dark as to why, since neither Ryan nor Rachel has ever expanded on why their relationship didn't work out.

At least 2007 ended on a positive note – Ryan found out he had been nominated for the 65th Golden Globe Awards for his work on *Lars And The Real Girl*. He had been nominated for the category of Best Actor in a Musical or Comedy. However, the award would go to Johnny Depp for his work on Tim Burton's *Sweeney Todd*.

The Golden Globe nomination was just one of a slew of award nominations for Ryan's work in the film, though. He would also receive nominations for the Screen Actors Guild Awards (Outstanding Performance by a Male Actor in a Leading Role), Chlotrudis Awards (Best Actor), Chicago Film Critic Association Awards (Best Actor), Prism Awards (Performance in a Feature Film) and the Broadcast Film Critics Association Awards (Critics Choice Award Best Actor). There were also award wins, too. Ryan won the Best Actor in a Motion Picture, Comedy or Musical at the 2007 Satellite Awards; the Cinema Vanguard award at the 2008 Santa

Barbara International Film Festival and a second-place Best Actor award at the 2008 Central Ohio Film Critics Association Awards.

Despite the critical kudos continuing to mass about *Lars And The Real Girl*, Ryan was suddenly adrift. He had been completely blocked out to dedicate the coming months to *The Lovely Bones* and had, of course, spent the past summer growing a dense beard and devouring ice cream for the role. That was all over now. And that meant he was abruptly faced with an unplanned for open schedule.

CHAPTER TWENTY-ONE

MOSTLY
GOOD THINGS

A s looked likely to happen, his pulling out from *The Lovely Bones* forced a sabbatical of sorts – at least in terms of films featuring Ryan Gosling to reach our cinema screens. There would now be a three-year gap between *Lars And The Real Girl* opening at cinemas in October 2007 and a new film called *All Good Things* opening in December 2010 – even if the time in between would see Ryan working as prolifically as ever.

In real terms, this was hardly a sabbatical – Ryan was attached to a new film project in less than ten weeks – and, in January 2008, it was announced that he was to star in *All Good Things*, a film set to be directed by Andrew Jarecki, who had come to attention with his acclaimed debut *Capturing The Friedmans* (2003).

All Good Things was written by Marc Smerling and Marcus Hinchey, who had also worked with Jarecki on

Capturing The Friedmans, and told the story of a wealthy heir to a real estate empire, David Marks, and his ill-fated marriage to a young woman, Katie McCarthy, who hails from a less affluent social background.

Ryan would take on the lead role of David Marks. Playing opposite him as Marks' wife, Katie, would be Kirsten Dunst, whose recent credits at the time included *Marie Antoinette*, *Spider Man 3* and *How To Lose Friends & Alienate People*.

Ryan had been involved with a class-crossing plot like this before – *The Notebook* – only then he had played the character from the less comfortable family. In this film, he would be the son born into a phenomenally wealthy and powerful family and test out the reverse perspective.

At first glance, *All Good Things* sounds like one of those classic Romeo and Juliet stories, in which David's father disapproves of his marrying a woman from the wrong side of the tracks and tries to break them up. Instead, David ignores his father's wishes and goes ahead and marries Katie. Thereafter, the story turns pitch dark, leading up to the mysterious events of Katie's disappearance.

The screenplay was based on a real-life story. Back in 1982, the heir to a significant New York real estate empire was suspected of allegedly killing his wife, but never tried, after she went missing and couldn't be found. Andrew Jarecki had become fascinated by the tale and researched it intensely, to the point that he all but made a documentary about it. He had tracked down everybody connected to the story and, where possible, filmed them telling their version.

In another inversion of a prior role, as David Marks, Ryan

also had the chance to move into Anthony Hopkins' character's predicament in *Fracture* and play the suspect, rather than prosecutor.

Before the shoot started, Ryan and Dunst undertook eight weeks of rehearsals. This mostly consisted of the two actors talking extensively about the screenplay, where it needed to go and how this story related to the one it was loosely based on. They also looked at footage shot by Andrew Jarecki as he investigated the story. This was useful for both Ryan and Dunst, who found it helped them to get a detailed grasp of the story and the characters they were playing. Dunst set out her intention from the start that she saw it as vital that she should not play Katie as a victim. She didn't want audiences feeling as though Katie was a woman who naively walked into a dangerous relationship, otherwise the film would lack any sense of suspense.

The film started shooting in April 2008, on location in Connecticut and New York, with a budget of $20 million. Ryan and Dunst worked well and intuitively together. This connection proved helpful when the time came to shoot a disturbing scene in which David has to drag Katie by the hair across a room.

Dunst later told the *Express Tribune* that Ryan found it really hard to perform this scene: 'The next day Ryan sent me flowers because he felt bad for having to pull my hair.'

As a man who grew up with his mother and sister, and who credits that feminine home life with having made him the man he is, it's easy to see why he would have found such a scene unbearable to shoot.

Ryan sending flowers as if he needed to somehow apologise for his work as an actor is very similar to his reaction at the end of *The Believer* audition, when he was also upset by the work he had just done and felt the need to apologise to the casting director for the offensive things he had just said in front of her.

By the time the shoot ended in July, Ryan was under scrutiny in the gossip columns as speculation mounted that he and Rachel McAdams had got back together. The rumours started after the couple were spotted at the Green Door Lounge club in Hollywood, where Ryan was trying his hand at DJ'ing for the first time.

There were other sightings that summer, too – the main incident being when Ryan and Rachel were spotted having breakfast together in Toronto, near where McAdams lived. The reunion wasn't to last long, though, and, by December, it seemed they had once more broken up. Most reports speculated that the break-up was down to struggling to make their relationship work against the backdrop of their combined busy schedules.

By this time, Ryan was becoming something of a cult icon on the internet. A single topic Tumblr had been launched by a fan called Douglas Reinhardt, in California, called *Fuck Yeah! Ryan Gosling*. He got the idea while stuck at home with a nasty case of bronchitis. Although his Tumblr initially launched only with postings of photographs of Ryan, it soon started to feature photographs accompanied by captions that always began with the catchphrase 'Hey Girl'. There is no reason why he chose the phrase 'Hey Girl' other than he thought it sounded good. Over the next two years, the Tumblr would become popular and inspire a tidal wave of 'Hey Girl'-inspired Tumblr memes and derivative blogs.

Some of the best and most popular examples include *Shakespearean Ryan Gosling*; *Hey Girl, I Like The Library Too*; *Silicon Valley Ryan Gosling*; *Real Food Ryan Gosling*; and *Feminist Ryan Gosling*, which became a 2012 book called *Feminist Ryan Gosling: Theory From Your Favorite Sensitive Movie Dude*.

As 2008 ended, Ryan (who was now 28) turned his attention towards music. As ever, he was keeping the fans guessing – this time, the surprise was coming in the guise of an interlude dedicated to making music.

CHAPTER TWENTY-TWO

DEAD MAN'S BONES

Ryan announced his forays into the realm of music with characteristic minimal fuss, on Christmas Day 2008, when a music video for a song called 'In The Room Where You Sleep' sneaked its way onto the internet. Simultaneously available as a free download, the artist was Dead Man's Bones. Spearheading this musical project: Ryan.

The video, which was shot live in what appeared to be a recording studio or rehearsal space, showed Ryan sitting playing a piano, wearing a tie, waistcoat, white shirt and cheap Casio watch, and singing, while another man – also in a white shirt and black tie – thumped out a primitive beat as a children's choir sang along with them.

Standing against a backdrop of garlands of lights and a wall painted to resemble a theatre set, the choir were dressed as if it was Halloween and variously dressed as mummies, skeletons, ghosts, werewolves and monsters. At the end of the video, a boy charges across the room, raises a sword and brings it down for a final crash on the cymbals – before running back to high five a mummified girl.

The song sounded like a mixture of Screamin' Jay Hawkins, Howlin' Wolf, Tom Waits, Nick Cave, Tindersticks and Arcade Fire, thrown together into a gothic blender. Ryan sang it in a low Roy Orbison-inspired croon, as if he was belting out a soundtrack to an imaginary 1960s horror flick.

And that's how Ryan revealed how serious he was becoming about music, with this video sneaking its way onto the internet and quickly coming to the attention of fans eager to hear what his band was like.

If that one-off release seemed exactly that, then Ryan was quick to dismiss this as an actor dipping his toe into another field. He and his musical partner, Zach Shields, opened 2009 by giving their first interview about their band, Dead Man's Bones, to the music industry title *Pitchfork*. In it, they revealed the extent to which they were taking Dead Man's Bones very seriously.

They explained that they had started making music after meeting in 2005. At the time, Ryan was, of course, dating Rachel McAdams and, by coincidence, Zach Shields was dating Rachel's sister, Kayleen. Through dating the sisters, Ryan and Zach were thrown into socialising together.

Zach, it turned out, was a theatre actor and that gave the two men an instant connection. Added to that, it turned out they were both heavily into music and quickly discovered they

Hollywood's cutest couple: Ryan and Rachel at the 13th Annual Screen Actors Guild Awards 2007.

© *Startraks photos/ Rex Features*

Above: Ryan entertains co-star Anthony Hopkins and his wife at the after-party for the LA Premiere of *Fracture* in 2007.

© Getty Ima

Below: Outstanding Performance nominee pours himself a well-earned drink backstage at the TNT/TBS broadcast of the 14th Annual Screen Actors Guild Awards 2008.

© Getty Ima

ars rubbing shoulders.

bove left: Deep in conversation with the revered Sir Ben Kingsley at the *Blue Valentine*
m reception in 2010 (Soho, London).

© *Richard Young/Rex Features*

bove right: Re-united with former co-star Kevin Spacey at the 16th Annual Critics'
*h*oice Awards 2011.

© *Getty Images*

ottom: Showing Steve Carell who's boss at the New York premiere of *Crazy, Stupid*
ove, in 2011.

© *Gregory Pace/BEI/Rex Features*

LA stroll: filming scenes for *Gangster Squad* in 2012.   © *On Location News/Rex Featu*

e reluctant Sgt. Jerry
ooters: Ryan stares
nsively into the distance on
e *Gangster Squad* film set.
Startraks photos/Rex Features

Above top: The all-star cast of *Crazy, Stupid, Love* at the film's world premiere in New York City in 2011. From left to right: Marisa Tomei, Julianne Moore, Steve Carell, Ryan Gosling and Emma Stone.

© Getty Ima

Below left: Gosling and Clooney are all smiles at the Beverley Hills premiere of *The Ides of March* in 2011.

© Getty Ima

Below *right*: Ryan congratulates Nicholas Winding Refn for his "Best Director" win for *Drive* at the 64th Cannes Film Festival 2011.

© David Fisher/Rex Featu

Above left: Posing with current actress and model girlfriend, Eva Mendes, at the Toront
Film Festival 2012.

© *Sipa USA/Rex Featu*

Above right: 'Mom Date': Ryan brings his mother Donna to the LA premiere of
Gangster Squad in 2013.

© *Broadimage/Rex Featu*

Below: Ryan face to face with himself, signing a female fan's painting at the *Gangster
Squad* premiere.

© *Getty Ima*

shared not only a lot of similar tastes in music, but also a mutual obsession with Disney's Haunted Mansion ride. Added to the mix, the pair also bonded over a shared love of The Cure, 1950s doo-wop music and both the 1964 Disney album *Chilling, Thrilling Sounds Of The Haunted House* and the 1969 *The Story and Song from the Haunted Mansion.*

The way they met may also have sparked a discussion about the 1978 cult album *Sister Lovers*, by Big Star – so named because Alex Chilton and Jody Stephens of the band were dating sisters. So, Ryan and Zach coming together with a shared love of music through the McAdams sisters slotted them into a fantastic musical lineage.

Ryan and Zach made the decision to start a band in 2006 while out on a road trip to Las Vegas to celebrate Mandi Gosling's 30th birthday. After that, the duo began putting on small shows for their girlfriends, family and friends. Ryan told *Rolling Stone* that the first of these shows was staged in a bathroom: 'We'd go in the shower and we'd use the shower curtain as the stage curtain.' Their friends and family thought they were kidding around, but Shields explained to *Rolling Stone* that it was the opposite: 'They would laugh afterwards and be like, "That was so funny!" And we'd be like, "We weren't kidding."'

Developing the idea further, they decided to set about creating an alternative theatre show – one which would blend music and theatre together in a vintage, vaudeville way.

They told *Pitchfork* that the plan had been to create a show packed full of spooky themes and characters – monsters, ghosts, zombies and so on – so that it was like the Haunted

Mansion ride married to a macabre work of theatre, married to the eclectic, surreal bombast of a later Tom Waits' album such as *The Black Rider*.

Despite plenty of ideas for shows, the two found themselves eventually drifting more towards writing music and, from there, they grew increasingly excited about staging the songs they were writing in the same sort of spooky, theatrical fashion. And that's how the idea for a play became an idea for an album. However, the only obstacle in the way of their writing and recording an album was quite a large one: neither one of them was a particularly gifted musician.

Over 2007 and 2008, they set about writing an album and, with that, figuring out how to play different instruments. To their surprise, the entire process would take two years. This had a lot to do with the kind of music they wanted to make and because they wanted to play every last instrument themselves.

Learning each instrument sufficiently to be able to lay down a track in a studio became an enjoyable, if laborious, learning curve. For instance, wanting to use a cello on the song 'Buried In Water' meant Ryan having to learn how to play the cello. But they weren't being stubborn or bloody-minded, quite intentionally they were doing this so they didn't have to hire a roll call of professional musicians. It was crucial to the sound they were after that the music should sound naive and un-manicured, and that wasn't going to happen if they brought in session musicians.

In the background of what they were doing were two albums that served as a template for the atmosphere, sound and feel they were after. The first album was Nancy Dupree's *Ghetto Reality* and the second was Langley Schools Music Project's *Innocence and Despair*.

Originally released by Folkways back in 1970, the Nancy Dupree album featured the artist performing songs she had written on the piano with the choir at a school she taught at in Rochester, New York. The Langley Schools Music Project album had the same idea – a Canadian music teacher called Hans Fenger recorded songs with students in the Langley school district of British Columbia during 1976 and 1977, only he chose to have them perform cover versions of classic songs. For instance, Fenger leads a choir through a version of The Beach Boys' 'God Only Knows'.

Fenger's efforts were originally released as two obscure albums: *Lochiel, Glenwood, and South Carvolth Schools* in 1976 and *Hans Fenger/Wix-Brown Elementary School* in 1977. In 2001, the albums were rediscovered and reissued by Bar/None records but as a single-volume anthology under the title *Innocence & Despair*. The album quickly became a cult word-of-mouth hit.

What Ryan and Zach liked about these albums was their yearning, improvised, near-kitsch, homemade feel, as well as the fact that the school choirs had that special naive charm that is unique to children's choirs. What they wanted to do was make an album that married the sound and feel of those two projects to the spooky Haunted Mansion ride melodrama of their earlier aborted theatrical show.

Both albums were a seminal, driving inspiration behind the kind of music Ryan and Zach wanted to make: music made in collaboration with a children's choir. As they began to gather material for a prospective album, the plan was to have all the vocals sung by a children's choir. But then, when they were writing songs, they found themselves singing the lyrics and, out of that, they decided to find a way to have the songs become duets between them and whichever children's choir they ended up hooking up with.

When the time came to start developing the songs, they found a perfect choir to work with: the Silverlake Conservatory Children's Choir, who were the house choir of the Silverlake Conservatory of Music in Los Angeles. As an added bonus, they were right on Ryan's doorstep, since he had recently moved from Downtown Los Angeles to the nearby then trendy neighbourhood of Silverlake.

The Silverlake Conservatory of Music was founded by Flea, the musician best known for being the bassist in Red Hot Chili Peppers. He set up the school on hearing that his former high school's music department had been significantly cut in terms of instruments and programmes from when he was a student. Flea founded the Conservatory with a view to offering a basic musical education to children between the ages of seven and seventeen, who could not get this at their own schools. Once it was set up, the Conservatory was eventually able to offer 250 low-income students a scholarship, through which they could attend free music classes.

To have access to working with the children, it turned out that Dead Man's Bones could only get together, write and explore music on Sunday afternoons. This was the only time when everyone could fit the project into their schedule since most of the children in the choir were busy with school throughout the rest of the week. So, for that reason, Dead Man's Bones would jam and sometimes record together, every Sunday, for many months on end. When they reached their final Sunday session, they shot the video for 'In The Room Where You Sleep' – the video sneak released on Christmas Day – as a document of their wrap party, which would feature, among other things, a piñata, a bouncy castle and even a taco track.

Ryan was constantly mesmerised by how adaptable and intuitive the children in the choir were. No matter what he and Shields threw at them – and these were macabre songs with equally macabre lyrics – they not only understood what he and Shields were aiming for, but they also helped to push the music to the next level. When asked by a reporter if the children ever found his and Zach's lyrics too dark and sinister, Ryan told *Pitchfork* that the children had the exact opposite reaction, telling him and Shields that 'It wasn't weird *enough.*'

Now it was time to make a record, which meant Ryan and Shields needed a producer. The logical choice was Tim Anderson, of the Los Angeles band Ima Robot, whom Ryan had met at a party in Los Angeles, where Anderson was DJ'ing. At the party, Anderson had played a bit of both of the Disney Haunted Mansion albums during his set and that instantly endeared him to the actor.

Now there were three people in their little music gang who loved that obscure, cult classic. Anderson would not only end up producing the debut album by Dead Man's Bones, but he would also form an independent record label – Werewolf Heart Records – with Ryan and Shields.

For the recording process, Ryan and Zach decided to keep things as natural as possible, which meant that, if they made a mistake, they'd keep the take rather than record a new take in search of a polished, perfect sound. This became an almost manifesto-like process whereby they set down a rule that they'd never record more than three takes of any one track – which meant that, even if they tried the same part three times and it didn't sound right, they'd have to stick with it. As well as the earlier rule that they would play all the instruments themselves, they also decided that they would never use a click-track to stabilise rhythm. If anything, they wanted the complete opposite: an organic, natural rhythm.

The *Pitchfork* article reported that the debut album would be released on Werewolf Heart Records and that they were in the middle of mixing the album, which, at the start of 2009, had the working title *Never Let A Lack Of Talent Get You Down*.

Jumping ahead to 4 April 2009, the band released another music video for their song 'Name In Stone' on MySpace and YouTube. The track featured the Los Angeles Inner City Mass Choir, as well as the Silverlake Conservatory Children's Choir.

Co-directed by Ryan and Shields, the black and white video was shot in a cemetery on 8mm film and has the feel of an old silent movie. As Ryan plays guitar and sings, Shields bangs a tambourine against his leg. Meanwhile, a woman slowly dances, clutching a baby, to their right, as children sit in the trees. Eventually, Ryan and Shields start walking as they're playing and singing, leading the choirs behind them like a funeral procession, among the graves and through the cemetery. Eventually, they finish the song by singing in front of a tomb, which is flanked by two people standing with white sheets draped over them. They resemble the ghosts in that old Abbott and Costello film *Hold That Ghost*, which Ryan had loved so much as a child.

In parallel with all this musical fun, Ryan was getting ready to shoot a new film. At the end of 2008, he had received a phone call from director Derek Cianfrance, telling him the great news that, finally, he had the backing to make a film he had long wanted to make called *Blue Valentine*. The actress Michelle Williams, with whom Ryan had previously worked in *The United States Of Leland*, had been attached to the project for several years, even longer than Ryan. She was still on board, despite having gone through the tragedy of the death in January 2008 of her former partner, actor Heath Ledger, with whom she had a daughter, Matilda Rose.

Ryan had been committed to making *Blue Valentine* since 2005, when Cianfrance first approached him, as he told *W* magazine, 'For four years *Blue Valentine* would be ready to go, and then the film would fall apart again due to financing or timing. It was always me and Michelle [Williams] – I think Michelle was involved for five or six years.'

In fact, this was the only film project spectacular enough that it was capable of dragging him away from his commitment to Dead Man's Bones.

CHAPTER TWENTY-THREE

BLUE VALENTINE

L ike *Half Nelson*, *Blue Valentine* would be a film that would underscore Ryan's seriousness as an actor and the increasing depth of his skill in a new way. The movie told the story of a couple's relationship, from their first meeting through giddy love, through marriage and then on to having a child and eventually estrangement. It was an ambitious project and one that its writer-director had wanted to make since he first started work on the screenplay, back in 2001.

Derek Cianfrance was born in 1974. He made his first films when he was 13 years old and later studied Film Production at the University of Colorado. When he was 23, he made his first feature film, *Brother Tied*, which met with acclaim after it premiered at the Sundance Film Festival in 1998.

Cianfrance started writing *Blue Valentine* when he was 27. He was using the screenplay to work through his feelings about his parents, who were madly in love when they had him and then, much, much later, ended up getting divorced. He told *Filmmaker* magazine, 'When I was a kid I had two nightmares: one was nuclear war, the other was that my parents would get a divorce,' and that, later, when his parents did divorce, he didn't know what to do with that scenario at all: 'Yeah, when I was 20 they split up. It was so confusing to me that I decided to confront it with a film and just started writing it.'

As he tried working through those feelings, for the next decade, he'd plough his way through 60 drafts of the screenplay, as he kept refining what he wanted to say.

In 2003, he had first approached Michelle Williams and talked her through the kind of film he was trying to make. He explained that he had written *Blue Valentine* to try to make sense of their break-up.

Williams, who was 21 at the time, understood where Cianfrance was coming from, and read the screenplay, connecting deeply to it. She later explained to *Marie Claire* magazine, 'I'm a child of divorced parents and it's a film about what it's like to grow up in that kind of atmosphere of tension and decay. Being forever in the pre-trembling of a house that falls.'

With Williams committed to the project, Cianfrance powered on with the screenplay, with one eye on the question of which actor might work best opposite his female lead. The idea of casting Ryan Gosling came to him in 2005. He told *Filmmaker* magazine that he knew Ryan was also a child of divorce, so he would get the story as poignantly as

Michelle Williams had. 'When finally Ryan and Michelle became a part of it they too are children of divorce, and they eventually became what I considered to be co-writers on the film. I worked with Michelle for maybe seven years on the film and with Ryan for about five. They never sat down with me at the computer to write, so to speak, but I would have countless meetings with them that would inspire the movie and the characters.'

By the time Cianfrance had secured financial backing, the film almost went back on to indefinite delay again because Michelle Williams, still traumatised by Heath Ledger's death, didn't want to be separated from her three-year-old daughter, Matilda Rose. She told the *Daily Telegraph*, 'I promised her that I'd take her to school every morning and tuck her into bed every night, and that we were going to stay in one place. So I had to call Derek back and through tears say, "I'm sorry. I can't believe that after all this time I have to let it go, but you have to cast somebody else."'

Racking his brain for a solution, since in his mind only Michelle Williams could play this role, Cianfrance went back to her with a proposition: would she accept the part if he could guarantee she'd be there for her daughter in the morning and at the end of the day? Williams was astonished that the director was actually proposing to reconfigure his entire location plan to suit her and said of course she would do the film, on that basis. Cianfrance went away and came up with a new list of locations that were all within an hour's drive of Williams' home in Brooklyn, New York, and she, in return, signed on to make the film.

With an estimated $1 million budget and Ryan Gosling and Michelle Williams on board as Dean and Cindy, with eight-year-old Faith Wladyka cast as their daughter, Frankie, they were ready to shoot on location in Brooklyn and, later, in Scranton and King of Prussia in Pennsylvania. The shoot lasted 30 days, with a month-long break in between, where some extraordinary rehearsals took place.

Using 16mm film, Cianfrance shot the falling-in-love and early days' scenes first. To achieve maximum authenticity, he arranged it so that Ryan and Williams would not meet until their first scene together when, as Dean and Cindy, they also meet for the first time. This meant that, aside from a single dinner in the run-up to making the film, Ryan and Williams spent no time rehearsing or mapping their parts out at all. Their coming to the roles of Dean and Cindy – all the figuring out of their parts and how they'd interact and play together – would be captured raw as it played out, on film, as Ryan told *Den of Geek*: 'Over the years that we were prepping our characters, Michelle and I never met. We'd had one dinner. So, when we showed up on set, we really met each other on camera, in character. So, when something's happening for the first time for the audience, it's really happening for the first time for us as well.'

When they finished shooting all the falling-in-love scenes and the month's break began, Cianfrance had Ryan and Williams move into the place that was to serve as the location home for the duration of the film. He asked that they live together as if they were Dean and Cindy, so that they'd get used to being in each other's space, as well as their likes and dislikes, habits and behaviours. The only concession was that they didn't have to actually share a bed in the house.

To take this character immersion still further, Cianfrance worked out with Ryan, Williams and the crew members what a house painter at Dean's level would typically receive as an annual income and what a nurse at Cindy's level would be paid. From that, they worked out what their monthly income would be. As a final calculation, Ryan and Williams were allotted a fortnightly food budget of $200. With that money, they were expected to go food shopping together and to buy basic everyday toiletries and so on. When the money ran out, it ran out, and they had to make do with what they had.

They'd also cook and eat in this temporary home and take turns in doing the dishes, too. Williams told the *Guardian* how Ryan had a natural tendency to take care of her during this leg of the shoot: 'Ryan's a great cook, he's really good at improvising. He said something sweet when we were in that rehearsal period. He did a lot of the cooking and a lot of the dishes, and I think finally I said to him, "Ryan, this isn't how it goes. This doesn't feel real to me." And he said, "I know, Michelle, but you have a home and a kid. You're cooking when you go home so I feel bad making you do it here too."'

Scenes like this were exactly what Cianfrance wanted – to have his actors be authentically synched in every way possible before they began shooting the half of the screenplay that would deal with their relationship starting to fall apart in the present tense. To ensure the present-tense and flashback scenes were easily distinguished, he made the decision to shoot the present-tense scenes using digital film and the flashback scenes using 16mm, so the older scenes would have a grainy quality and the present-tense scenes would be crisp.

In the scene at the start of the film when Dean wakes up, Ryan was waking up in real life, too. He had fallen asleep in the living room one night and Cianfrance had the crew tiptoe in and start filming him. Such was the degree to which the director strived for utter realism.

Cianfrance had always talked of the film as being a duet that would take place on the screen, between Dean and Cindy – a man and a woman – and that duet would be the story of their meeting and falling in love and then having to reframe their love, day by day, as life and the world impacted on them and chipped away at their love, little by little. To get the results he wanted, Ryan and Williams sometimes had to go through a relentless number of takes. For the scene where they are taking a shower together, Cianfrance couldn't get the take he wanted, so he kept them doing and re-doing it until they had been in the shower, washing themselves and saying their lines, for two full days. Only by that stage, with both actors at breaking point, did he see in their performance the exact take he wanted.

In another scene, where Dean is hard at work as part of a removal company job, Cianfrance actually auditioned real-life removal company teams until he found the right fit. He then had Ryan join them in their work as they carried out a real-life job, moving *Blue Valentine*'s cinematographer, Andrij Parekh, from his East Village apartment to his new home in Park Slope, Brooklyn.

Being such a gritty, realistic film, it's no wonder that Cianfrance named it *Blue Valentine* after the 1978 Tom Waits' album of the same name. He told *The List* that he named it in 'homage' to Waits. Ryan, also being a massive Tom Waits fan, must have loved this reference and would have known the album that Cianfrance was referring to intimately.

Williams told the *Daily Telegraph* that shooting the film brought her back to life after Heath Ledger's death: 'It was my first experience of work being fun in a long, long time. Especially during the first part of making the movie, the falling in love part. That was the beginning of feeling myself again for the first time in a long time. I had forgotten.'

For Ryan, it was a return to the kind of project he adored: a film that simply had to be made by everyone involved. It took him back to that epiphany when he was 14 and watched *Blue Velvet* and came away feeling reverence and awe that David Lynch had felt compelled to make such a work and had no intention of compromising any part of his vision.

When the shoot was complete at the end of June 2009, Cianfrance undertook a painstaking editing process, during which he screened the film privately close to two dozen times, on every occasion carefully considering and then responding to the feedback of each select audience.

Though Ryan came away from working on the film, he found it hard to break the intense spell that Cianfrance had created. He would later tell the *Guardian* that he didn't know how to come back to himself after the shoot: 'Most movies when you're acting you're trying to block out the lights and the trailers. Here, you had to remind yourself you were making a film. Michelle and I found it hard to take off our wedding bands when it was over. We'd built this castle and then had to tear it down.'

CHAPTER TWENTY-FOUR

ON TOUR

With his work on *Blue Valentine* complete, Ryan threw himself into a hectic upcoming schedule that revolved mostly around Dead Man's Bones. Not only did the band have an album due later in the year, but they were thinking of going out on a short tour, too.

Ever mindful of global issues, Ryan found time in May 2009 to serve as a panel judge for a YouTube contest titled *Come Clean 4 Congo*. This was an initiative between Ryan's friends at the Enough Project and YouTube. People were asked to make videos, which 'create compelling messages that highlight the link between conflict minerals used in cell phones and the war in the Democratic Republic of the Congo'.

A panel of judges featuring Ryan, the filmmaker Wim Wenders and actress Sonya Walger (best known at this time for her work in the TV show *Lost*) watched many entries and then, on 23 July, the three semi-finalists picked by the panel were announced and the public were invited to vote. Matt Smith was announced as the winner on 9 September and received his award on 24 October at the Hollywood Film Festival's Human Rights Symposium.

At the turn of July 2009, news broke that the Los Angeles-based record label Anti Records had signed Dead Man's Bones to an album deal. For Ryan, a key factor in the choice of label must have been that they were home to one of his favourite songwriters, Tom Waits.

In September that year, Ryan and Zach Shields, keen to go about every aspect of being in a band differently to the usual way of doing things, put out an open call seeking local entertainers who might be interested in being considered as opening acts for an upcoming Dead Man's Bones tour across the US. The advertisement asked for unconventional performers with unusual talents and requested that would-be hopefuls send in DVD or VHS demos. That same month, the band staged a trio of shows, accompanied by the Silverlake Conservatory Children's Choir at the Bob Baker Marionette Theater in Los Angeles on 11, 18 and 25 September. The theatre, which can be found at 1345 W. 1st Street in the Echo Park neighbourhood of Los Angeles, was founded by puppeteer Bob Baker and his business partner, Alton Wood. The pair bought the venue, which had previously housed a special effects workshop, in 1961 and converted it so they could re-open it as a children's marionette theatre in 1963.

It was the perfect venue for a Dead Man's Bones residency. Reviewing the middle date, *LA Weekly*'s reporter enthusiastically wrote, 'The band itself was not the centerpiece of the night; blurred into the background, it was the engine driving the multimedia performance that tipped a hat to 1950s rock and grade-school performances'.

On 17 September, Dead Man's Bones released a new video called 'Hypnotism'. It was a promotional trailer for the imminent release of their debut album. Equal parts Hammer Horror, *Ed Wood*, Tim Burton, 1960s horror B-movie, *The Twilight Zone*, David Lynch and Michael Jackson's 'Thriller' video, the promo features a special effects stricken ghostly face floating out of darkness, talking in a Halloween-like way, before the clip ends in less than two minutes with the band's name and the release date of their debut album flickering onto the screen in a kitsch style as if these are the credits to a low-budget horror movie.

The promotional trailer was directed by Ryan and Shields. Animation was by Leah Ordonia, a Los Angeles-based designer, illustrator, animator, artist, writer and director. *The Twilight Zone*-referencing warbly, spooky, theremin-soaked music is credited to Eban Schletter and Alexander Burke. Schletter, a composer and songwriter, is well known for his skills on the theremin. For the video, Burke played the vibes. The Vincent Price-esque voiceover was provided by Daamen J. Krall, an actor who has also lent his distinctive voice to many TV shows and films.

The band's eponymously titled album, *Dead Man's Bones*, was released on 6 October 2009 and attracted positive reviews. Ryan must have been nervous of rock critics going for the jugular, perhaps sensing the project had the potential to be an actor's vanity project. But like Scarlett Johansson's musical outings – a year before Dead Man's Bones put out their own debut, she had released a well-received album, *Anywhere I Lay My Head*, almost completely filled, bar one track, with sublime cover versions of Tom Waits songs – Dead Man's Bones found their own album met with surprised, glowing reviews.

Pitchfork's reviewer summed up the album's achievement as being that it managed to shout down any issues it had, so that it eventually triumphed: 'I'm as surprised as you are with Dead Man's Bones. So many ways for it to go wrong, but instead it's a unique, catchy and lovably weird record.' *Spin* magazine also liked the record saying, 'At its best, the duo's debut shambles along like a Tom Waits-led, Tim Burton-produced Halloween recital.' And *Q* magazine shared *Pitchfork*'s surprise that the album was actually good, concluding: 'Incredibly, it works.'

Ryan later very succinctly described what they were trying to do with the music they were making, in an interview with *New York* magazine in summer 2010, saying: 'The music is spooky doo-wop.'

In support of the album, Dead Man's Bones headed out on a two-week-long tour in October 2010. As a precursor to the full tour, they played a warm-up show at the Bob Baker Marionette Theater on 9 October and then launched the actual tour in Boston, Massachusetts, at the Middle East, on 14 October.

Spin magazine reviewed the opening night, which was sold out. Focusing on Ryan's role, the reviewer noted, 'Gosling switched between piano, percussion, acoustic and electric guitar and his voice purred like a '50s crooner.'

The local choir, which featured ten children dressed in the by now expected Dead Man's Bones spooky costumes, supported Ryan and Shields, who were joined by Andye Jamieson, a flute and piano player. Considering the rapturous applause coming from the audience, *Spin*'s reviewer asked, 'Sycophantic celeb-loving? Or respect for Gosling's musicianship? Bit of both, seemed like.'

The band then moved on to play dates in New York (Le Poisson Rouge), Philadelphia (the First Unitarian Church sanctuary), Washington, DC (Sixth & I Historic Synagogue), Montreal (Le National) and Toronto (The Music Gallery), before arriving in Chicago for two shows on 21 October at the Schubas venue. The final leg saw them play in Seattle (The Triple Door), Vancouver (Venue), Portland (Mississippi Studios) and San Francisco (Swedish American Hall), before bringing the tour to a climax in Los Angeles, at The Regent, on 30 October.

At every date, Dead Man's Bones had a different, local choir waiting to work with them and venues had to be alternative to the usual 'band' venues because the children's choirs necessitated the booking of sites that would not enforce age restriction.

As the tour ended, Ryan stepped back into actor mode, in time for the premiere of *Blue Valentine* at the Sundance Film Festival on 24 January 2010. He and Michelle Williams were present for the screening, which was held at the Racquet Club Theatre. Blessed with positive reviews, the film also caught the attention of Harvey Weinstein, whose company, The Weinstein Company, acquired distribution rights before the festival came to an end.

CHAPTER TWENTY-FIVE

MEETINGS & OPPORTUNITIES

As per the organic rhythm of his acting career, which by now assumed a pattern of full-throttle intensity followed by an interlude enjoying a new kind of non-acting creative challenge, Ryan came out of his musical sabbatical by attaching himself to the lead role in a film called *Drive*. It was set to be directed by Nicolas Winding Refn, whose previous work included the *Pusher* trilogy, *Bleeder*, *Bronson* and *Valhalla Rising*.

The movie, an adaptation of the 2005 novel of the same name by crime writer James Sallis, had been considered as a potential project since 2008, but it wasn't until Danish director Winding Refn became interested in making the film that it came alive as a project.

It was not the type of film Ryan was usually attached to – after all, at first glance, it appeared to be an action movie. But the producers saw the story as being the kind of film that would have previously starred Steve McQueen and they felt that Ryan could easily play the part with the same icy internalised mystery as McQueen conjured up so brilliantly for the 1972 action-crime film *The Getaway*. Those attached to the project were also thinking of how Ryan O'Neal played the getaway driver in *The Driver* (1978) and Alain Delon the hitman in the 1967 French film *Le Samouraï*.

The first time that Ryan and Winding Refn met, the meeting was not a typical first meet between a director and the potential star of his next film. Ryan had apparently invited Winding Refn, whose work he admired, to dinner so they could talk over the possibility of adapting Sallis' novel into a film.

Ryan in turn had been engaged in the project by producer Marc Platt, as he told *Movie Fanatic*, 'Marc Platt [producer] gave me this script and said, "Do you want to produce it with me?" and then any director I wanted, he would support. So, I had to find the right director.'

Having flown into Los Angeles, Winding Refn arrived in the throes of coming down with an attack of flu, which he believed he had caught while travelling. Subsequently, by the time he and Ryan made it to dinner, he was feeling under the weather and distinctly groggy from the medication he had taken to temper the symptoms, so he wasn't saying an awful lot. Halfway through dinner, Winding Refn decided he felt too ill to carry on and said he needed to go. Ryan didn't object to cutting the dinner short at all. By this stage, he wasn't really enjoying himself and was even concerned that he might have signed up for the wrong film. To make matters worse, he then asked if Ryan could drive him home as he didn't hold a driving licence. Ryan understandably panicked further, later telling a reporter, 'I'm thinking, how can this guy make a movie about driving and he doesn't even drive!'

As Ryan drove Winding Refn home, still barely connecting, REO Speedwagon's 1984 single 'Can't Fight This Feeling' came on the radio and the director started singing his lungs out and apparently crying as well. Suddenly, Ryan saw a completely different side to the filmmaker. At the end of the song, he apparently turned to him and said, 'This is it! It's a movie about a guy who drives around listening to music.' Ryan had been thinking the same thing. In that sudden click between the two of them, the project was salvaged, as Ryan later recalled to *Movie Fanatic*, 'This movie wouldn't have happened if REO Speedwagon hadn't come on the radio when I was driving Nicolas home from our first terrible meeting. The movie wasn't happening. It was a bad meeting. It was a bad date – no one was getting any action. So it was just get out of the car, go home.' By the end of that night, Winding Refn and Ryan had resolved to make the film together.

Although Ryan had attached himself to this project, *Drive* was not the next film Ryan would be shooting. First, he was about to make a movie that would serve as a kind of palette cleanser between the intensity of shooting *Blue Valentine* and *Drive*. Of all things, it was to be a super mainstream romantic comedy, albeit an extremely well-written one: *Crazy, Stupid, Love*.

Talking to *Collider* in 2011, Ryan explained very succinctly how he came to sign up for a major role in a light-hearted rom-com: 'When I finished *Blue Valentine*, I had to go get a physical from the doctor and he gave me a prescription and it said, "Do a comedy."'

As ever, he was thinking strategically. If *The Notebook* had shown his versatility and *Half Nelson* underscored how he could burn up a cinema screen in the way Marlon Brando used to, fans and critics were now poised to expect him to go one way or the other: a romantic turn or another of his trademark dark, intense roles. Instead, he flipped both expected routes out the way and signed himself up for a comic role – the last thing anyone would expect from Ryan Gosling.

As ever, he wanted variety and a challenge, and this new film would offer him exactly that: he'd need to convince large, mainstream audiences who regularly went to see movies such as the one he was attaching himself to that he could be funny. And the question that went with this career move was obvious: could an actor so cool, so serious, so intense, pull it off?

CHAPTER TWENTY-SIX

CRAZY, STUPID, LOVE

Written by Dan Fogelman, who had previously penned screenplays for films such as *Cars*, *Fred Claus*, *Bolt* and *Tangled*, *Crazy, Stupid, Love* was set to be co-directed by Glenn Ficarra and John Requa, who had previously worked as a team co-writing among others *Cats & Dogs* and *Bad Santa*. They had also co-directed *I Love You Phillip Morris*.

The story was about a suburban couple, Cal Weaver (played by Steve Carell) and Emily Weaver (Julianne Moore), who suddenly reach a crisis point in their marriage. Out of the blue, Emily announces that she is leaving Cal, who finds himself suddenly flung back out onto a singles scene he no longer understands. To help get back out there, he seeks advice and counsel from a man he meets at a bar – Jacob Palmer – a serial bachelor and ladies' man, who can seemingly pick up any woman he wants. As the two set out to find Cal some new female company, Jacob finds his bachelor life under threat when he meets and falls for a beautiful young law student, Hannah, played by Emma Stone.

The co-screenwriters and directors were obviously well aware that Ryan did not have a background in comic acting, that he was known for his unrelenting intensity and commitment to acting, but, still, they had a gut instinct that told them that he would bring so much to the part of Jacob Palmer. So they sent him the screenplay, without any high level of expectation.

Next thing they knew, they heard Ryan was indeed interested and, when Ficarra and Requa met with him, they found him to be not only very funny but also someone with whom they really got along well. Within a short period of time, he was signed to the film.

There was, of course, a high level of risk for Ryan that some of his diehard fans would see him taking a part in such a movie as a sell-out manoeuvre. But he overrode this because he loved the sound of the film and the part, and, just as importantly, he was a big fan of Steve Carell. He was also stepping into a lineage of many serious actors who wanted to challenge themselves by taking a comic turn onscreen – for instance, Marlon Brando undertaking any number of comic roles during the 1960s.

At the heart of the role as well was the opportunity for Ryan to gently satirise the pin-up status with which *The Notebook* had labelled him. It would allow him to luxuriate in that perception of him, while simultaneously giving him scope to send up the image (and himself) with it. To prepare for the part, he turned to a friend who owned a bar in Downtown Los Angeles called Varnish and asked him to teach him how to make various cocktails and drinks – he felt this was an important aspect of getting into character if he was to play a man like Jacob Palmer.

He read a lot of men's magazines, absorbing advice on how to dress, exercise tips that would give a man the optimum appearance and general pointers on how to woo and seduce women. He also read the bestselling 2005 book *The Game: Penetrating The Secret Society Of Pickup Artists*, by journalist/author Neil Strauss, in which Strauss set out to see what he could learn from some of the slickest pick-up artists. To complete his preparation, he watched the VH1 reality TV dating game show *The Pickup Artist*.

The film, which had received a green light in December 2009, went quickly into pre-production in January 2010 and began shooting in April of that year. It was made quickly, over a 54-day shoot.

Many scenes were hilarious for Ryan to shoot, in particular the scene where he and Cal appear in a locker room. Ryan had to play the scene so he would be standing stark naked before Steve Carell with Carell's head protecting his modesty from the camera. Carell then had to play it as if Cal was trying very hard not to look at Jacob's penis, while the two are talking. But, of course, he can't stop looking at it because it's right there, in his face! Ryan later admitted he found the scene excruciating to shoot. Steve Carell told *thereelbits.com* that the scene cracked them up: 'It was so hard not to laugh. We giggled all the way through it. I had the idea that maybe my character should pass out and maybe fall forward toward him, which he had to prepare himself for both physically and emotionally.'

Ryan adored working with Steve Carell. They had briefly worked together before when both appeared on the abandoned TV pilot *The Unbelievables* (1999). As before, Ryan felt good around Carell and the finished footage shows him looking at all times as if he was having a lot of fun making the film.

Of course, many fans would later wonder if Ryan's take on Jacob Palmer was autobiographical in any way; if Ryan – as a successful, talented actor who turned so many women weak at the knees – was somehow also this bachelor-slash-ladies' man. When asked about this in interviews, Ryan laughed it off, saying he wasn't at all like Jacob but instead a lot like Cal, and that he was attracted to the role because it gave him the opportunity to play someone who was the polar opposite of what he was really like.

Aside from working with Steve Carell, Ryan also enjoyed working with Emma Stone, who would play Hannah, the character who breaks Jacob's well-oiled act in two and leaves him ready to check out of his bachelor life and into a proper committed, romantic relationship. Ryan told *Collider*: 'I knew the movie was going to be good when she signed on. The whole thing really hinges on her character; my character has to give it all up for her and that has to make sense. Show me a man who wouldn't give it all up for Emma Stone and I'll show you a liar.'

Crazy, Stupid, Love was originally slated to open at cinemas in April 2011, but, when they saw early cuts, Warner Bros became very excited and decided to move the release date back to summer 2011, so that it could take to the stage as a major summer movie. During that time, the co-directors were allowed to keep tweaking the film until they felt it was perfect.

Meanwhile, Ryan was doing anything but resting. He flew out to France with Derek Cianfrance and Michelle Williams for the screening of *Blue Valentine* at the Cannes Film Festival on 18 May. In photographs taken there, he posed with his arm around Michelle Williams, which added fire to speculation that had been mounting since the film premiered at the Sundance Film Festival about whether the actors had carried on their onscreen relationship when the movie wrapped.

As stories about the extent to which the pair were encouraged to go to authentically depict Dean and Cindy's story – in particular, the month Cianfrance had them live together for live rehearsals – became public knowledge, naturally fans, critics and gossip columns wondered if working so closely, especially since both actors were believed to be single at the time of the shoot, had inevitably sparked a romantic connection in real life.

Though Ryan and Williams didn't go out of their way to deny they were a couple, they certainly said nothing to confirm anything was going on. Appearing on the ABC *News Nightline* show in December 2010 together, they were asked what they thought of each other, and Ryan said Williams was like 'Brigitte Bardot meets Clint Eastwood, she's like a cowboy, a sexy cowboy'. They were then asked whether the rumours about their relationship carrying on off-screen were true and Ryan replied, 'Creatively, we are doing it – creatively,' which caused him and Williams to giggle nervously. The interviewer probed deeper and asked if at any time they had been dating, to which Ryan said, 'No, we're professionals.' Although that appeared to be the literal answer – they were not a couple – their cute nervous giggling together only led to another round of 'are they/aren't they?'

Ryan had also lent his voice, for a second time, to a documentary project. *ReGeneration* was written and directed by Phillip Montgomery. The film, which used the Occupy Movement as a gateway to taking the pulse of contemporary social activism and, by contrast, socio-political apathy within young American people, premiered at the Seattle International Film Festival on 24 May 2010. With a soundtrack by STS9, it would screen again at the Edmonton Film Festival on 26 September 2011, before formally being released much later, on 4 May 2012.

On Ryan Gosling's narration and his coming on board as a producer, the director told *Variety*: 'As a socially conscious individual himself, Ryan brings an inspired freshness to the film's core message of hope and action.'

Meanwhile, refusing to let the musical momentum he had built up fade away, that summer Ryan kept his hand in with Dead Man's Bones. The band played a short residency at the Eagle Rock Center for the Arts in Los Angeles on Saturday, 26 June, Sunday, 27 June and Saturday, 3 July 2010. They performed with the Silverlake Conservatory Children's Choir.

In August, Magnolia Pictures announced they had acquired rights to *All Good Things* and were scheduling the film for a December release. Given that the project had been in the pipeline for a long time, Ryan was likely pleased to learn that it was now going ahead.

That autumn, he began work on *Drive*. By then, he was telling interviewers that, the way he saw the film, it would turn out as a 'cross between *Blue Velvet* and *Purple Rain*'. The combination was pretty startling: on the one hand, that dark, sinister, troubling David Lynch film; on the other, a near-operatic piece that served as a gloriously indulgent platform for pop superstar Prince.

By this stage, Ryan and Nicolas Winding Refn, who had secured a $13 million budget for his film and a screenplay written by Hossein Amini, were very excited about working together and very in sync about the kind of film they planned to make. Their flu-stricken 'bad date' of a first encounter was long since history.

A key influence that they both felt needed to serve as a backdrop to the work they were doing were the teen films made by John Hughes in the 1980s, such as *Pretty In Pink*, *Some Kind Of Wonderful*, *Sixteen Candles* and *The Breakfast Club*. Ryan later elaborated on this in an interview with *Total Film*, saying, 'Both Nicolas and I felt that if *Pretty In Pink* had a head-smashing scene, it would be a masterpiece. The only thing missing from John Hughes's movies was violence.'

Continuing that line of inspiration, Winding Refn cast Carey Mulligan as Irene, the driver's next-door neighbour, who is unhappily married to a convict, because she reminded him of a 'young Molly Ringwald' – a favourite actress of John Hughes – who appeared in *Pretty In Pink*, *Sixteen Candles* and *The Breakfast Club*.

Ryan and Winding Refn also started to think of *Drive* as a quintessentially Los Angeles film in its dreaminess, its car-obsessed cool, the poetry of driving around the city ad nauseam... But then they began to worry if that overarching theme would translate to audiences who had never been to Los Angeles and knew nothing of how the city's entire population is slave to the car. To get around this, they started thinking of the basic plot – of the driver moving towards falling in love with his next-door neighbour, Irene – in terms of mythology. They decided Ryan was to approach his character as if he were a knight and Mulligan would act as if she were a princess trapped in the tower and in need of rescue.

For preparation over the summer, Ryan had taken stunt-driving lessons with a real-life stuntman called Darrin Prescott. They would meet in parking lots and practise and practise, driving old Mustangs until Ryan could handle all kinds of elaborate and complex manoeuvres. On top of that, for the actual film, Winding Refn told Ryan to buy any car he felt would be right for the character. Ryan purchased a broken-down 1973 Chevy Malibu for $2,000 and then challenged himself to restore the vehicle to roadworthy condition. He prided himself on being able to restore and repair every part and element of the car – the only thing he didn't do was fit a new transistor: a mechanic took care of that.

Winding Refn and Ryan both loved the 2002 film *Irreversible* by Gaspar Noé and felt that *Drive*'s violent scenes would be great if they came even close to matching the intensity of Noé's movie. They wanted to have a scene where there was a head smashing but they weren't sure how to go about it, so Winding Refn contacted Noé to ask how he went about doing that scene in *Irreversible*. Noé talked him through the process.

Once shooting began, Ryan asked Winding Refn to remove more and more of his lines. It was a textural decision – to work with fewer words would challenge him to express his character in non-verbal ways. He wanted to play the driver with an almost Zen-like silence so that, when he speaks, it carries power.

To finalise the details of the role, Ryan selected what he believed was the perfect jacket for the driver – one with a large scorpion design on the back – and went to painstaking lengths to settle on the right kind of toothpick to chew on: choosing in the end a brand which are prepared in tea tree oil. As ever, he was assessing his character holistically and making sure that every aspect and detail of his personality was in place before the cameras started to roll.

Ryan told *Total Film* that he carried on his onscreen mysterious, wordless, staring demeanour with Carey Mulligan even when they weren't shooting: 'Carey and I, our relationship off camera was very similar to our relationship on camera. We really just kind of looked at each other. It just felt good. I just liked looking at her. And I didn't want to blow it by saying anything.'

In building this character, Ryan was taking his acting ability to a new level. With less emphasis on verbal acting, Ryan was exploring a new physical dimension, which he loved, as he told *Screenrant*: 'On a more practical level I had just come off of doing *Blue Valentine* and on there I improvised and just talked, talked, talked, talked, talked. I had to promote it and I just talked, talked, talked and I was just tired of my own voice, with talking in general. I felt like the more I talked, the less I felt like I was saying. So we just went to set everyday [for *Drive*] with this and just removed all the dialogue that wasn't absolutely necessary.'

Beyond that, Ryan was working flat out, taking on a rush of parts that he felt intensely connected to. He had no plan to conquer Hollywood; he had just entered a period when a surprising number of parts that he wanted to play had come to him. This meant, for once, he was forgoing his by now customary sabbaticals and, as a result, his films were queuing up for release, meaning that Ryan Gosling's name and face were suddenly going to be plastered across multiple film posters all over the world.

CHAPTER TWENTY-SEVEN

OBSTACLES & MILESTONES

olding up the release of *Blue Valentine* was a harsh censorship ruling in October 2010 from the Motion Picture Association of America (MPAA), who had slapped the film with an NC-17 rating – a certification that would severely restrict the potential audience. The MPAA's ruling had come about after they objected to the scene where Dean performs oral sex on Cindy, deeming it too sexually explicit.

The Weinstein Company were very surprised by the rating and made it known, promptly launching a campaign to have the MPAA reverse their decision. They had no intention whatsoever of asking Derek Cianfrance to cut the offending scene.

Meanwhile, Ryan turned 30 on Friday, 12 November 2010. He kept details of how he celebrated fiercely private. But it is known that the next day, on Saturday, 13

November, he took his mother with him to the Academy of Motion Picture Arts and Sciences' Governors Awards ceremony, a film industry event, at the Grand Ballroom of the Hollywood and Highland Center. Then, on Sunday, 14 November, he went to Disneyland. It made sense that he should include the park in his celebrations, since, over and over, he returned to Disneyland, this near-sacred place in his psyche. By tapping into those Mouseketeer days when he would spend his free time taking the Haunted Mansion ride, he was always able to reboot and set himself back to zero. What better way, then, to mark a milestone birthday, such as his 30th?

Mindful of how lucky he had been in his career, it also seemed logical that he should pay back some of that good luck by doing something good for a group of children that day. In photographs of Ryan wandering about the park, wearing a baseball cap, sunglasses, faded black jeans, a grey V-neck T-shirt and grey cardigan, with a badge clipped on the cardigan that read 'Happy Birthday', he was in the company of a group of children, to whom he was giving a VIP tour (who the children were has not been disclosed).

Immediately after his birthday, Ryan took off to the Eastern Congo, once more with Enough Project's John Prendergast, to see the effects of the ongoing conflict in which armed groups fight to secure finds of precious minerals that can be sold on to companies manufacturing cell phones and laptops. The pair spent much of their time talking with victims of the violence – women who had been subjected to rape, and those displaced from their homes because they had been located near lucrative mines. Documentary footage shot on the trip became a short film that Ryan made titled *Raise Hope For Congo*. He and Prendergast would later co-write an opinion piece posted on *The Huffington Post* on 27 April 2011 under the headline 'Congo's Conflict Minerals: The Next Blood Diamonds'.

Once back from the Congo, Ryan made the decision to leave Los Angeles and move to New York. The move was perhaps inspired by his 30th birthday, a way of marking the milestone, of shaking things up.

One of the main reasons for the move was that he wanted to be closer to people, to street life. As an actor, he needed such stimuli – the palette of faces on a street, the random experiences that happen in a densely populated city like New York. He said he was tired of spending his entire life in a car in Los Angeles, negotiating traffic and car-parking issues; he wanted to be in a city with a strong street life, where life played out on the pavements and there was always something happening or an interesting face walking past you or sitting beside you. '[It was] something to do, as I had just turned 30,' he told *Radar*. 'But also, in Los Angeles, it's easy to lose touch with everything. You just sit in your car the whole time. In New York, you're forced to deal with life, it's there in front of you on a daily basis.'

After what had felt like a relentless wait, *All Good Things* finally opened in cinemas on limited release on 3 December, taking just $37,172 over its opening weekend. Not helped by mixed reviews, the film would go on to gross just $644,535 worldwide. At the same time, the censorship drama dogging *Blue Valentine* came to a head and, in early December 2010, the MPAA bowed to pressure and reversed the earlier NC-17 rating, downgrading it instead to an R certificate. The good news reached Ryan just as he finished work on *Drive*.

As 2010 drew to a close, Ryan spoke with *The Los Angeles Times* and told them how he felt about having two films – *All Good Things* and *Blue Valentine* – coming out near simultaneously: 'I get sick of myself, so I can imagine how everyone else feels. And for the two to come out at the same time, it makes me feel sick.'

Of course, it had nothing to do with Ryan that both films were coming out in this way and, as he said, he felt overexposed having two performances go out into the world at the same time.

After giving his all in *Blue Valentine*, he must have been holding his breath to see if Cianfrance's film would connect with audiences. Having been a steady presence throughout 2010 at many prominent international film festivals, the movie opened in the US as a limited release on 29 December and took $193,728 over its opening weekend.

In the weeks that followed, positive reviews helped the film open its reach. The *Observer* underscored Ryan's and Williams' performances, saying, 'Both Williams and Gosling give excellent, detailed performances, at once spontaneous and carefully considered, playing people who cannot understand or properly articulate their position,' as did *The New York Times*, whose reviewer wrote, 'Ms. Williams and Mr. Gosling are exemplars of New Method sincerity, able to be fully and achingly present every moment on screen together.'

Such reviews, coupled with the gossip that excitedly

questioned whether the onscreen couple were an off-screen couple too, helped *Blue Valentine* to start pulling audiences in as it opened more widely in the New Year.

CHAPTER TWENTY-EIGHT

ARE THEY,
AREN'T THEY?

A s *Blue Valentine* began to take off in the US, it also opened on 14 January 2011 at cinemas in the UK, igniting a fresh round of speculation on both sides of the Atlantic as to whether or not Ryan was dating Michelle Williams.

The 'are they, aren't they?' question followed them even more doggedly as the pair promoted the film. The fact that the speculation had been going strong for nearly a year and showed no signs of dying out was testimony to the film's power. As had happened with *The Notebook*, audiences were seemingly struggling to see the couple portrayed in *Blue Valentine* as Dean and Cindy, and not Ryan Gosling and Michelle Williams. Cianfrance had so expertly erased the boundary between real life and film that everyone was genuinely confused and reacting as if the movie really was the candid documentary of a relationship he hoped it would appear to be.

Of course, beyond that, there was a simple daydream fantasy scenario at play that imagined Ryan and Williams as making a cute couple. With Williams having been through the tragedy of losing former partner Heath Ledger, gossip columns loved the idea that Ryan might have stepped in to take care of Williams as she worked through her grief.

When Ryan went on Ellen DeGeneres' talk show that month, she said outright that she thought he and Williams made a cute couple. Putting him on the spot, she added that, while she didn't know if they *were* a couple, if they happened to be one, she would be thoroughly behind the idea. Ryan laughed off her train of questioning, but did not say outright that the rumours were untrue, causing the speculation to reach a whole new level.

He also fanned the flames again while talking about the contentious censor-baiting oral-sex scene with the *Guardian*. Going over why he thought the scene had courted so much drama with the censors, when a similar episode between Natalie Portman and Mila Kunis in Darren Aronofsky's *Black Swan* had not, Ryan said that in his opinion it was down to the authenticity of the way the scene was shot. 'The sex felt real,' he told the newspaper. 'It wasn't sexy or a sex scene, and that's why we got into trouble.'

The film courted a new round of attention in the run-up to the 68th Golden Globe Awards ceremony, which was to be staged at the Beverly Hilton Hotel on 16 January. Back in December, Ryan had found out that he had been nominated for a Golden Globe for his performance in *Blue Valentine* in the Best Performance by an Actor in a Motion Picture: Drama category. He was up against stiff competition in the form of Colin Firth for his work in *The King's Speech*, Jesse Eisenberg for *The Social Network*, James Franco (*127 Hours*) and Mark Wahlberg (*The Fighter*).

For the ceremony, Ryan turned up looking very Cary Grant, very old Hollywood, in a tuxedo, black shoes and a black velvet bow tie. In red carpet interviews that he and Derek Cianfrance did together, Ryan stressed that *Blue Valentine* was a small film, made on a small budget and that they didn't have a huge Hollywood-style promotional budget, which meant that the Golden Globes nominations – Michelle Williams had also been nominated in the Best Performance by an Actress in a Motion Picture: Drama category – had given the movie the gift of a high level of 'free' publicity, something the makers of a small film can only dream of. When it was time for the Best Performance by an Actor in a Motion Picture: Drama award nominees to be announced, it was read out by Sandra Bullock. The camera zoomed in on Ryan, who was sitting with Derek Cianfrance – the pair were by now close friends. Bullock then read out the winner – the award would go to Colin Firth for his performance in *The King's Speech*.

Although anticipated, Ryan did not receive an Academy Award nomination for his work in *Blue Valentine*, but his and Michelle Williams' nomination for Best Performance brought Cianfrance's film welcome publicity.

The Golden Globe nomination was just one of many accolades to be presented to Ryan for his work in *Blue Valentine*. He won the 2011 Chlotrudis Best Actor award for his performance and also picked up many other nominations including the Critics Choice Award for Best Actor at the 2011 Broadcast Film Critics Association Awards; the CFCA Best Actor award at the 2010 Chicago Film Critics Association Awards; the Actor of the Year award at the 2011 London Critics Circle Film Awards and the Best Actor in a Motion Picture, Drama award at the 2010 Satellite Awards.

With the award nomination buzz, combined with all the speculation about Ryan and Michelle Williams' off-screen relationship, interest in *Blue Valentine* snowballed. The film went on to take $12,355,734 worldwide, making it both a critical and commercial success.

CHAPTER TWENTY-NINE

SPECULATION & HEROICS

The year 2011 was shaping up to be an incredibly busy one. Ryan's fans and critics had grown accustomed to his rising up to a certain level of attention and then pulling back from the spotlight's glare. After the spotlight shone on him with *Blue Valentine* and with *Crazy, Stupid, Love* due to be released in the summer, this was usually when Ryan concentrated on making music or went to Africa, or took a head-clearing job in a sandwich shop or decided to open a Moroccan restaurant. But this time, he would choose a different tactic: instead of stepping out of the tornado of attention that was fanning up about him and promising to blow him up to an even higher profile in his career, he would go with it and set his attention on taking more acting parts and exploding his potential with what was about to become the most prolific period of his entire career to date.

The first of his new roles was in *The Ides Of March*, a new film project to be directed by the actor/producer/writer/director George Clooney. Having already established his credentials as a director with *Confessions Of A Dangerous Mind, Good Night, and Good Luck* and *Leatherheads*, Clooney had his latest script set in the murky world of politics and was scheduled to begin shooting in February 2011.

The film was adapted from the 2008 play *Farragut North*, by Beau Willimon. Willimon wrote the play based on his own experiences of working on a presidential campaign in 2004 and adapted his work into a feature film screenplay in collaboration with George Clooney and writer/producer/director Grant Heslov, who co-owns Smokehouse Pictures with Clooney.

Renamed *The Ides Of March*, the movie would tell the Shakespearean backroom story of a Democratic Presidential candidate, Mike Morris, the current Governor of Pennsylvania, whose campaign to triumph over another Democratic Presidential hopeful hits some turbulence due to a scandal in his private life.

Clooney was not only directing, but also starring in the film as Mike Morris, the Presidential hopeful. On top of that, he was, of course, also co-screenwriter and co-produced the film with his business partner, Grant Heslov, and, among others, the actor Leonardo DiCaprio – making his role that of an ambitious four-hander. Originally, he had it in his mind to shoot in March 2008, but, given the storyline, he decided to postpone the project when Barack Obama was elected US President in November of that year. A sceptical political drama, especially one concerning Democrats, would be out of step with the jubilant mood among Americans after Obama's victory, he felt. In time, of course, he figured the theme of dirty politics, image manipulation and ruthless personal ambition could easily become poignant again once Obama's honeymoon period came to an end. That time had now come around, and, with an estimated $12.5 million budget, the film went into production.

Ryan had been cast as Stephen Meyers, Mike Morris's junior campaign manager. In the film, Ryan's character engages in a power struggle with his boss, senior campaign manager Paul Zara (played by Philip Seymour Hoffman), and drifts into a wrecking-ball scenario of a fling with an intern, Molly Stearns (Evan Rachel Wood), working for Morris.

As Ryan was busy shooting *The Ides Of March*, he was suddenly romantically linked to the actress and model Olivia Wilde, after a member of the public filmed the pair enjoying a visit to an aquarium in Cincinnati close to where he was shooting. When the footage was posted online, a round of media speculation broke out about whether the actress, who had recently announced her separation from her husband, Tao Ruspoli, was now dating Ryan. Or were they were just hanging out as friends? News stories noted that Ryan and Wilde had also been seen talking at The Weinstein Company's 2011 Golden Globe Awards After Party, back in January. However, neither has ever commented on the episode and the rumours quickly disappeared.

Not long before, rumours had also circulated that Ryan was dating the actress Blake Lively, after they were seen at

Disneyland together, eating ice cream and enjoying the park, in October 2010. Then further speculation broke out after they were spotted at the New York premiere of *Blue Valentine*. As with the Wilde rumours, neither made any comment about why they were spending time together and the rumours they were dating also died out as quickly as they began.

Now that Ryan was considered an extremely high-profile actor, naturally it came with the territory that he had to contend with a high level of scrutiny over his private life. It seemed that any woman he spent time with was automatically cued up as a possible new girlfriend.

Meanwhile, on 20 May, *Drive* premiered at the Cannes Film Festival. Ryan showed up at the screening in a blue tuxedo, white shirt, black bow tie and a healthy dose of designer stubble. On the red carpet, he appeared relaxed and posed for photos with director Nicolas Winding Refn.

Reviews were unanimously positive for the film, with most critics honing in on how captivating Ryan's almost wordless performance is and drawing comparisons between his performance as the driver and the acting style of Clint Eastwood, Steve McQueen, Paul Newman and Lee Marvin. *Variety* applauded Ryan's career shift, saying of his performance, 'After serving up a pair of intense, emotionally draining performances in *Blue Valentine* and *All Good Things*, Gosling swings to the other extreme with *Drive*, channeling Alain Delon's cipher-like hitman from *Le Samourai*,' while the *Guardian* zoomed in on Ryan's 'charisma and presence'.

With *Drive* collecting positive reviews and *Crazy, Stupid, Love* set to open at the end of July, it hardly seemed that Ryan needed any more good publicity, but a story spread across the internet about how Ryan apparently stepped in to cool down a dispute between two men on St Mark's Place in Manhattan, New York. A bystander had started filming the argument and, to her surprise, she suddenly found herself filming Hollywood's Ryan Gosling, who appeared in exercise clothes, put down his shopping bags and waded in to bring a halt to the heated dispute. Most reports state that the incident took place on 24 June, but no one outside of the immediate scene knew Ryan was involved until a clip of his breaking up the clash appeared on YouTube on 22 August, and instantly went viral.

This incident was the first of a number of 'Knight In Shining Armour' episodes in which Ryan would find himself involved. Some nine months later, he would intervene in another New York scene when a British woman came perilously close to being knocked over by a New York taxi. That incident, which became notorious after the woman he saved – a journalist by the name of Laurie Penny – tweeted on 3 April 2012 that Ryan Gosling had saved her from an oncoming car, would further mythologise his heroic streak, portraying him as the kind of man who would think nothing of diving in to stop an argument or to save a damsel in distress. Each time one of these incidents occurred, his status as a Hollywood heartthrob was turned up a notch among his female fans.

CHAPTER THIRTY

THE PLACE
BEYOND
THE PINES

That summer, in July 2012, Ryan went back to work with *Blue Valentine* director Derek Cianfrance. This was the first time he had worked a second time around with the same director. Many actors work over and over with a director with whom they click, the shorthand between both growing ever more poignant with each season of working together. Notable examples include Robert De Niro's relationship with Martin Scorsese, Johnny Depp and Tim Burton, and Joaquin Phoenix's pairing with James Gray.

Cianfrance and Gosling were about to begin shooting a new film called *The Place Beyond The Pines*. This particular shoot would be longer than *Blue Valentine*, but still fast – 46 days – although this time there was a far larger budget, estimated at $15 million. The film was scheduled to shoot on location in

Upstate New York, predominantly in Schenectady, but also Glenville, Scotia and Niskayuna.

Written by Derek Cianfrance, with Ben Coccio and Darius Marder, the movie concerns a motorcycle daredevil stunt rider (Luke), who quits his life in a travelling carnival after they pass through Schenectady in Upstate New York and he discovers that his former girlfriend, Romina (played by Eva Mendes), has secretly had his child – a son named Jason.

Reunited with Romina, to support his new family, Luke takes a job as a mechanic. On learning of Luke's motorcycle stunt prowess, a colleague proposes they join forces and rob a bank. Believing the money will help his son to a better life, Luke goes along with the idea. When they put their plan into action, a rookie police officer, Avery Cross (Bradley Cooper), with his own wife, Jennifer (Rose Byrne), and son, AJ, comes after Luke. The film becomes a reflection of possible pathways for two fathers, each looking to give their son the best life they can.

The first draft was written by Ben Coccio while Cianfrance was busy making *Blue Valentine*. When Coccio finished, he had a 160-page screenplay, which he saw as being close in spirit to *Giant*, the classic 1956 film starring Elizabeth Taylor, Rock Hudson and James Dean. Once *Blue Valentine* wrapped, Cianfrance and Coccio went to work on the screenplay together, distilling the essence of the story and reducing the content until it was streamlined and concise. Cianfrance set the story in Schenectady because his wife had grown up in the small town, as had Coccio.

For the final stage of writing, which took place in early

2011, Cianfrance brought in Darius Marder to help with any last-minute touches. Marder, a friend of Cianfrance, also lives in Brooklyn and their children attend the same school. They would drop the kids off at school in the morning and then write all day, stopping only when it was time to collect them. During that stage, the fathers and sons' theme was turned up even higher and, by July, when Cianfrance was ready to start shooting, they were working with a screenplay that was the 37th and final draft.

Cianfrance later said the idea for the film was inspired by a moment in his own life: the impending birth of his second son. He was in a frame of mind where he was thinking about how he'd go about being a father this second time around and how the way he would do so would fit into the legacy and lineage of his ancestors. Out of that contemplation grew the idea for the film. As he later told *Movieline*, 'It's a movie about what we pass on.'

Before Cianfrance had even finished the script or mentioned it to Ryan, when the pair were talking, Ryan apparently said, 'I always wanted to rob banks, but I'm scared of jail!' This startled Cianfrance because he was deeply immersed in writing his new film and Ryan's comment chimed with that. Straight away, he told him about the new script and Ryan loved the sound of it.

Ryan was cast as Luke and, to play him, he learned how to handle a motorcycle in fast-paced scenes and how to do certain stunts, taking instruction from a rider named Rick Miller, who taught him a lot of key moves. He also bleached his hair blond and decided that Luke would be heavily tattooed – this character detail extended to Ryan having a teardrop tattoo design made up to go on his cheek. He also imagined Luke as being the kind of person who would always have a cigarette dangling from his lips so he built that into the character detail as well.

Just before they commenced shooting, Ryan made a last-minute decision to play Luke with a large dagger tattoo on his face. He told Cianfrance that, while it seemed to be right to add this extreme tattoo, he was concerned that it was excessive. Cianfrance heard him out and then told him that, if a person got such a tattoo on his or her face, then it would feel excessive, too much, that it would be endlessly there – in other words, totally definitive. Ryan liked this thinking and stuck to his intuition, which told him the tattoo was necessary.

The film locations were perfectly and authentically realised. Inbal Weinberg, the production designer in charge of this, had also worked with Cianfrance on *Blue Valentine* and shared his approach, which meant that, on both films, she would furnish and design rooms in a house they were shooting in, even if those rooms were not going to be used in the film at all. She felt it was vital that the actors had a sense of being in a fully materialised, authentic space rather than just working in staged rooms. Details associated with the characters would therefore permeate every part of a space they were shooting in.

When Cianfrance was shooting the motorcycle-chase scenes, he had in mind TV shows such as *Cops* and *America's Wildest Police Chases* – real-life, hard-to-believe, out-of-control episodes that happen in everyday life. Ryan did many of the stunts in the film, wanting to keep his character's onscreen performance as real as possible. But there were also stunts that he knew he could not handle and which he deferred to Rick Miller, who had, of course, coached him on how to handle a motorcycle for several months before shooting began.

To achieve trademark authenticity, Cianfrance tracked down a real-life convicted bank robber, who was fresh out of prison and spent time with him, soaking up his memories and stories. He also arranged for Bradley Cooper, Ray Liotta, Gabe Fazio and Luca Pierucci to spend time with the real-life Schenectady police department so that they could get a feel for their everyday lives – this extended to going out on duty with the officers. Harking back to the approach for *Blue Valentine*, on days when they weren't shooting, Cianfrance had Rose Byrne spend time in the location house with Bradley Cooper, so they could develop their performance as a married couple.

For Ryan, working again with Cianfrance was a chance for them to build on the rapport they had created during *Blue Valentine*. With that film having been so intense and detailed to make, he and Cianfrance had developed a catalogue of shorthand between them and this became their foundation for working on the new project and enabled them to take their commitment even further.

For the director, working with Ryan again was about things beyond the work itself. He fundamentally liked the actor, as he later told *Movieline*: 'He's just a magic person. He makes things better. We've all seen him save people from getting hit by a car, and we've all seen him break up fights in the city. And that's what he does in a movie. He makes the world a better place. He makes me a better filmmaker and everyone around him better.'

Cianfrance cast Eva Mendes as Romina. He had first become excited about her work after seeing James Gray's *We Own The Night* (2007). He began meeting with potential actresses who might work as Romina but, in the back of his mind, he was always thinking about Mendes. Finally, he sent the screenplay to her and invited her to come and audition. She apparently showed up wearing no make-up and dressed down. Cianfrance immediately sensed that she got the part and the film that he wanted to make. He spontaneously swore off a formal audition and instead asked Mendes to take him out for a drive. He said he wanted her to drive him around Los Angeles and to show him the old haunts where she grew up. As they drove around, the director saw a side of her that would be perfect for Romina. He told *Movieline* that the drive revealed 'this deep, thoughtful, warm, generous, and unpredictable person inside of Eva. She opened up about herself, her life, her past, and so I offered her the role.'

Cianfrance's hunch proved right and Mendes was incredible when they started filming. Her first scene was where she and Ryan have sex in a trailer. Cianfrance was surprised by how scared the actress was; Mendes was apparently trembling. The small crew tried to make themselves invisible so she and Ryan could shoot the scene. By the end of that first day, Cianfrance knew he had picked the right actress to play Romina. It would also prove fortuitous casting for the two actors, who became close during the shoot.

While Ryan was shooting *The Place Beyond The Pines*, *Crazy, Stupid, Love* premiered in New York at the Ziegfeld Theater on 19 July 2011. In photographs taken at the event,

Ryan was sporting stubble and wearing a slick patterned suit, white shirt and black tie. He looked relaxed and confident. Gone was the uncertainty and discomfort that he sometimes carried at premieres of his earlier films. Now he appeared focused and driven – and entirely ready for the career explosion that was about to happen.

CHAPTER THIRTY-ONE

WINNING STREAK

S wept on by advance hype and rave reviews, *Crazy, Stupid, Love* opened at cinemas in the US on 31 July 2011, taking a whopping $19,104,303 million over the opening weekend. This was set to be Ryan's first bona fide Hollywood blockbuster.

It would go on to take an enormous $142,851,197 at worldwide box offices. This was Ryan's *Pirates Of The Caribbean* moment, as *Crazy, Stupid, Love* showed that he could draw massive mainstream audiences, just as the first *Pirates Of The Caribbean* film had proved that Johnny Depp, after years of offbeat, intense roles, could also pull in the crowds.

The box-office success of *Crazy, Stupid, Love* also underscored Ryan's potential. Seemingly, he could appear in a romantic comedy just as successfully as he could take part in dark thrillers like *Murder By Numbers*, *Fracture* and *All Good*

Things or in intense, character portraits such as *The Believer, Half Nelson, Lars And The Real Girl* or *Blue Valentine*. Ryan was now at a point in his career where it seemed that he could appear in anything and make a success of it.

Adding to his suddenly exploding profile, on 31 August 2011, *The Ides Of March* premiered as the opening film of the Venice Film Festival. Generally, it was well received, gathering mostly positive reviews, especially for Ryan, who was not present. The *Guardian* wrote: 'It gained loud applause at its first screening, particularly for Ryan Gosling, who plays the idealist spin doctor. It would be a surprise if Gosling did not get an Oscar nomination for best actor.' The *Daily Telegraph* also saw Ryan as the central aspect of the film, writing, 'Despite Clooney's multi-tasking presence, Gosling takes the on-screen honours. There is a stillness and certainty about his acting, a commanding ability to convey complex emotions in the flicker of an eye.'

At the start of September, with *The Place Beyond The Pines* having wrapped, Ryan learned that he was to be awarded the New Hollywood prize at the Deauville Film Festival in France.

The following week, Ryan was back in Canada where *The Ides Of March* screened, accompanied by a press conference, at the Toronto International Film Festival, on 9 September. At the press conference, he looked laidback, wearing black trousers and a cream top over a green T-shirt, topped off by a long chain necklace as he took questions alongside Evan Rachel Wood and George Clooney.

On 18 September, Ryan's prolific breakout moment got even busier as *Drive* was released at cinemas. Over the past months, it had seemed as if his face was everywhere – in magazines, newspapers, on the internet, on film posters.

Drive took a healthy $11,340,461 over its opening weekend in the US and went on to gross $76,175,166 worldwide. Considering the film had an estimated $12.5 million budget, like *Crazy, Stupid, Love* it now constituted another commercial success for Ryan. Not only was he seemingly everywhere all of a sudden but also every one of the three films he had out (or about to come out) was a success.

Adding to his winning streak, that month he is believed to have started dating Eva Mendes. As had happened with Sandra Bullock and Rachel McAdams, Ryan met Eva while they were making a film together – in this case, *The Place Beyond The Pines* – and then got together with her after the film wrapped and several months had gone by.

It's interesting that a similar pattern was reported to have played out after *Murder By Numbers* with Sandra Bullock and then after *The Notebook*, with Rachel McAdams. Perhaps it's a case of professional integrity, whereby neither party wants to jeopardise the work itself by crossing professional and personal lines while working. Or, being so intense about the way he plays each character, maybe Ryan does not feel as if he is able to think outside of that realm while working.

Eva Mendes, like Sandra Bullock and Rachel McAdams, is older than Ryan. She was born to parents of Cuban descent on 5 March 1974 in Miami, Florida, making her six years and eight months his senior.

Mendes lived in Miami until her parents divorced, then she and her three elder siblings reportedly moved with their mother to Glendale, California. Raised in a Catholic home, Mendes said in one interview that, at one time as a child, her aspiration in life was to become a nun when she grew up.

Later, while studying Marketing at California State University, Northridge, Eva had a chance moment – a friend of hers was showing her portfolio to a casting agent and he saw Eva in one of the photographs and was instantly taken by her look. This led her to debut in several music videos.

She subsequently dropped out of Northridge to study acting at the Ivana Chubbuck Studio in Los Angeles. After a run of early roles, not dissimilar to Ryan's early TV parts, she came to attention when she was cast in *Training Day* (2001). This meant that her first significant film credit was in a hit Denzel Washington movie – just as Ryan's first feature film role had been in the hit Denzel Washington film *Remember The Titans*.

After finding success with *Training Day*, Mendes went on to underscore her talent and onscreen charisma with roles in films such as *All About The Benjamins, Hitch, Once Upon A Time In Mexico, Stuck On You, Ghost Rider, The Other Guys, We Own the Night, The Women* and *Bad Lieutenant*. She has also modelled extensively, often for social and political causes such as a Revlon breast cancer research campaign and for a PETA campaign. Mendes also volunteers regularly with the Art of Elysium, an organisation that matches artists with sick children, so the artist can go and perform for the child to raise their spirits. From 2002 until 2010, she was in a relationship with the filmmaker George Augusto, and lives in Los Feliz, Los Angeles.

In October 2011, it was reported that Mendes had visited

Sierra Leone to meet with rape victims. She was there to make a documentary that would draw attention to the victims, called *Half The Sky: Turning Oppression into Opportunity for Women Worldwide*. This trip, and its motives, chime with Ryan's own work in drawing attention to political events in Darfur, Uganda and the Congo that often fail to attract attention from the Western media.

The rumours that she and Gosling were dating began when Ryan took Eva to Disneyland on Saturday, 3 September. They were photographed hanging out and enjoying the park. Ryan was wearing a baseball cap, long chain necklace, sunglasses, a long-sleeve T-shirt and carrying a Marlon Brando in *On The Waterfront* checked lumberjack coat thrown casually over his shoulder, while Eva was wearing a grey top, Beatles cap hat, jeans and carrying a simple tote bag over her shoulder. In one photograph, they're walking holding hands. In another, she's pulling him close and kissing his cheek. And then, in a third, they're seen enjoying one of the many Disney attractions at the park. In all the photos, they look incredibly close and happy together. The mood is one of a cute couple. Apparently, the day ended with the couple checking out Tomorrowland at 10 o'clock in the evening.

By this time, Ryan had come straight off *The Place Beyond The Pines* to begin work immediately on a new film. He was keeping up the same relentless pace, with his career as an actor set to 'prolific'. The expected creative sabbatical that had become so commonplace in his career was seemingly not on the agenda during this time; he wanted to stay focused and on track, to prioritise his acting career. The results were stellar: a rash of spectacular films all shot back to back, all successful, all powering his name into the upper stratum of Hollywood's finest actors.

CHAPTER THIRTY-TWO

RISKS & ROMANCE

If Ryan wasn't taking any creative sabbaticals, he certainly wasn't choosing roles that were in any sense predictable. He could easily have taken another high-profile, mainstream comic role in the wake of the summer blockbuster success of *Crazy, Stupid, Love* or he might have chosen a romantic leading role, harking back to *The Notebook*, or he could have signed up for another independent. He took none of these pathways, though, and instead attached himself to a period gangster film called *Gangster Squad*.

The movie was to be directed by Ruben Fleischer, who had previously made *30 Minutes Or Less* (a series of short films) and directed for TV. The screenplay was written by Will Beall, who had worked on the TV series *Castle* – based on Paul Lieberman's *Tales from the Gangster Squad*. In turn, the book was based on a column Lieberman wrote for *The Los Angeles Times*.

The film was set in Los Angeles in 1949, at a time when a New York mob king called Mickey Cohen has extended his reach to control all kinds of criminal enterprises in the city. Via a wide network of corruption, he has many police officers and also local politicians under his control, too. Working against this vicious machine is a renegade unit of eight LAPD personnel called the Gangster Squad, who are eager to bring Cohen and his empire down. The unit operates without an office, without rules, with just one goal: to destroy mob activity in Los Angeles.

Ryan's character – Jerry Wooters, a sergeant in the Los Angeles Police Department – was the leader of this small police group, along with Sergeant John O'Mara (played by Josh Brolin). Mickey Cohen was to be played by Sean Penn. Cohen's classic gangster's moll, Grace Faraday, was to be played by Emma Stone – with whom Ryan had worked with so well in *Crazy, Stupid, Love*.

Ryan prepared for the role by meeting with relatives of Sergeant Jerry Wooters. He told *Screenrant*: 'We got a chance to meet some family members and his kids came to the set and they told me a lot of great stories. Like apparently when he ashed his cigarette, he would ash in the cuff of his pants. Then at the end of the day, he would dump out all the ashes in his cuffs.' In the same interview, he joked that he went about this role by pretending he was Humphrey Bogart.

He also worked on developing a voice higher than his own, so he played the role with a complete change in register.

Gangster Squad started shooting on 6 September 2011, with an estimated $60 million budget. It was filmed on location in Los Angeles, using, wherever possible, historical locations where real-life Gangster Squad incidents took place.

Later that September, taking time out from the shoot, Ryan was spotted taking a walk with Eva Mendes around the grounds of Griffith Observatory in Los Angeles, which is very close to her home in Los Feliz. According to *People* magazine, who covered the sighting and were able to quote a source who had additional insights: '[Ryan] visits Eva at her house as often as he can. The couple have enjoyed many quiet nights with delivery food.'

Following his appearance at the Toronto International Film Festival, on 27 September, Ryan attended the Los Angeles premiere of *The Ides Of March*. He turned up wearing a green Gucci suit, a white shirt and a tie and posed for photographs alongside George Clooney and other cast members.

Two weeks later, *The Ides Of March* opened on 7 October 2011 in US cinemas, taking $10,470,143, which meant it almost recouped the estimated budget of $12,500,000 over that weekend alone. It would go on to take $75,993,061 worldwide, connecting Ryan to yet another massively successful box-office success.

As his profile rose ever higher, his relationship with Mendes seemed increasingly serious. For Thanksgiving weekend, Ryan jetted off to Paris, where Eva was based at the time, shooting a film called *Holy Motors*.

The film, which starred Denis Lavant, was the latest by director Leos Carax, whose impressive credits include *Boy*

Meets Girl, *Les Amants Du Pont Neuf* and *Pola X*; it was his first feature-length effort in a dozen years. Eva had been cast as a character called 'Kay M'.

Ryan flew into Charles de Gaulle airport so they could hook up in Paris for a few days. The next day, he and Eva were photographed visiting the city's legendary Père Lachaise Cemetery, a large, village-like cemetery, where the graves of many celebrated artists can be visited, including Jim Morrison of The Doors, Oscar Wilde, Molière, Colette, Chopin and Edith Piaf.

Several months after this sighting, Eva told an Italian magazine, *IO Donna*, how grounding she finds cemeteries: 'I love graveyards and old churches, I find them peaceful and quiet. It all started 15 years ago when I first visited Père Lachaise in Paris. I don't pray though, I meditate.'

Ryan and Eva were captured in photographs strolling arm in arm among the graves. He was wearing sunglasses, faded black jeans, a black sailor-style winter coat and his usual heavy combats. In one photo, his right hand is shown bandaged up. They then went on to take a tour of the Catacombs of Paris. After the Catacombs trip, the pair visited the Eiffel Tower and ended up having what was reported to be a lengthy three-hour dinner at Le Jules Verne restaurant within the tower.

During his trip, Ryan turned up on the set of Carax's film and watched Eva shoot scenes with Denis Lavant by night. He was reported to have hung about on set and to have sat with her between takes. At one point, he was shown returning to the set carrying a plastic bag containing two cans of Red Bull, the energy drink. When that evening's shooting wrapped, he and Eva left together for a private dinner.

At the end of his whirlwind visit to Paris, Ryan flew back to the US from Charles de Gaulle airport. Photographs show him at the airport with Eva, walking hand in hand, Ryan managing to clutch Eva's hand and a paperback book, with the same hand – which was still bandaged – but it's unclear if they flew back together, or he flew back alone.

On 15 December 2011, the *Gangster Squad* shoot wrapped. Ryan had been working flat out all year and had made a staggering three films, back to back: *The Ides Of March*, *The Place Beyond The Pines* and now *Gangster Squad*. It was as if he had been in a feverish hurry to catch up with himself, perhaps to make up for lost time through his various acting sabbaticals when he seemed to need to step out of the Hollywood pressure cooker to catch his breath. Now, he seemed to have opted for a different approach and was totally focused on hard work, constant work, outstanding work. It was as if he had pressed his foot to the floor and planned to keep it there. Gone was the need to decompress or to ground himself by doing things like working in a sandwich shop. Like never before, he appeared focused on acting, and the scale of his energy and ambition was unstoppable.

The latest bolt of excitement came in the guise of nominations for the 69th Golden Globe Awards. Ryan had been nominated for the Best Performance by an Actor in a Motion Picture award for his work on *The Ides Of March*. He was up against Brad Pitt for *Moneyball*, his *Ides Of March* director George Clooney for *The Descendants*, Michael Fassbender (*Shame*) and Leonardo DiCaprio (*J. Edgar*).

Ryan's nomination was one of several for *The Ides Of March*, which had also picked up nominations for Best Screenplay, Best Motion Picture Drama and Best Director Motion Picture. To his surprise, he had also been nominated for a second category, too: Best Performance by an Actor in a Motion Picture – Comedy or Musical, for his performance in *Crazy, Stupid, Love.* For this award, he was competing against Jean Dujardin for *The Artist*, Owen Wilson (*Midnight In Paris*), Brendan Gleeson (*The Guard*) and Joseph Gordon-Levitt (*50/50*).

As if the double Golden Globes nomination wasn't enough, to round off the year, Ryan appeared in a short film called *Drunk History Christmas*, which premiered on *Funny Or Die* on 20 December. Co-directed by Derek Waters and Jeremy Konner and written by Derek Waters, the comic short – which saw comedian Allan McLeod play himself as he tries to recite 'The Night Before Christmas' after sinking a bucket of whisky – was the latest instalment in the ongoing *Drunk History* series.

To help McLeod make it to the end of the story, Jim Carrey, Eva Mendes and Ryan all pop up to encourage him to finish the classic poem. It was another comic turn by Ryan, following on from his first winning comic performance in *Crazy, Stupid, Love.*

It is also interesting to note that the fiercely private actor chose to appear in the film with his girlfriend, since he usually prefers to keep his private life far from the public eye. It was as if everything Ryan was doing was about becoming more comfortable and open, while his professional profile was going from strength to strength.

CHAPTER THIRTY-THREE

STAR IN
THE ASCENT

The year 2012 began with Ryan reuniting with *Drive* director Nicolas Winding Refn. After once again working with Derek Cianfrance, he was ready to join forces for a second time with Winding Refn, giving the actor two recurring collaborative credits with the same directors. It seemed he wanted to work with directors who knew how he liked to work, how he worked, what he was capable of, and who could push and challenge him, helping him to take his work to the next level.

Only God Forgives first came into being as a project back in 2009. The script, also by Winding Refn, tells the story of Julian, an Englishman who has lived in Bangkok, Thailand, for the past decade. After killing a police officer, he moves into exile there. In Bangkok, he runs a Thai boxing club with his brother. However, the club is a front for a drug-smuggling operation they run, which links up with their mother Crystal (played by Kristin Scott Thomas), in Florida. Julian and his brother are well known and respected within the Bangkok underworld.

After Julian's brother kills a prostitute, the police appoint a retired police officer called Chang – known as the Angel of Vengeance – to deal with the case. Suddenly, Julian's brother is found dead. Crystal flies out to Bangkok and demands that Julian should find out who has killed him and settle scores by killing that person in return. Julian then finds out that the police appointed Chang to kill his brother. This spirals into a showdown in which he challenges Chang to a boxing match – a fight that in theory will settle their dispute.

When Ryan was sent the script and offered the part, he thought it was unusual: 'It's the strangest thing I've ever read and it's only going to get stranger.'

From the start, Winding Refn had wanted to shoot on location in Bangkok, being an admirer of the city, which he has compared to being like a real-life *Blade Runner*. He told *Indiewire* how he imagined the film: 'From the beginning I had the idea of a thriller produced as a Western, all in the Far East, and with a modern cowboy hero. I was lucky – Ryan Gosling has accepted the role when Luke Evans withdrew.'

To get in shape for *Only God Forgives*, Ryan needed to undertake intensive Muay Thai martial arts training, and he studied with Kiu Puk, a Muay Thai master, at a centre in Studio City, Los Angeles. Muay Thai is a form of combat martial arts known as the 'Art of Eight Limbs' because it makes use of body parts other than the hands and feet – for instance, the elbows and knees. Training involved the pair working together four days a week, for sessions lasting two hours at a time. In tandem, Ryan needed to follow a traditional Thai diet of rice, fish and vegetables. He studied Muay Thai for four months until January 2012, when he was due to fly out to begin shooting on location in Bangkok.

In early January, when he was based in Bangkok, Ryan appeared at the opening night gala of the Hua Hin International Film Festival, where he was guest of honour. *The Hollywood Reporter* quoted him as saying, 'Ever since I came here I've been dreaming about making a film in Bangkok. I'm happy to be here.'

However, he was not able to attend the Golden Globe Awards ceremony on 13 January 2012 at the Beverly Hills Hotel. The media jumped on his no-show, trying to figure out why an actor in the throes of a gigantic breakthrough, nominated for no less than two awards, would not attend. George Clooney told the press that the reason was simple: Ryan was in Thailand working on *Only God Forgives* and so deeply immersed in his work that it was out of the question for him to break focus and take time out to fly to Los Angeles and then straight back to Bangkok after the awards. In any case, Ryan did not win either award. His *Ides Of March* co-star Clooney scooped the Best Actor award for his performance as a grief-stricken husband and father in *The Descendants*.

Ryan's work in *The Ides Of March* would give him another round of the by now obligatory award nominations, though. He was nominated for the AACTA Best Actor award at the 2012 Australian Film Institute Awards, the Critics Choice

Award for Best Ensemble Acting at the 2012 Broadcast Film Critics Association Awards and the COFCA award for Best Ensemble in the 2012 Central Ohio Film Critics Association Awards, as well as an actual win for the second place COFCA Actor of the Year award, also at the 2012 Central Ohio Film Critics Association Awards.

Shooting of *Only God Forgives* began in February 2012. Winding Refn had a budget believed to be $4.8 million. As had been the working method for *Drive*, the film was shot in chronological order and at the end of some days the director would go straight to editing footage. The shoot wrapped in April and Ryan headed back to Los Angeles, where he seemed to be spending most of his down time again.

Even if *Drive* was now firmly in the past, he was still collecting award nominations and wins for his performance: he had been given the Best Actor award at the annual 2012 *Empire* Magazine Awards; nominated for the Best Actor award at the Broadcast Film Critics Association Awards 2012; awarded second prize in the Best Actor category at the 2012 Central Ohio Film Critics Association Awards; nominated for Best Male Lead at the 2012 Independent Spirit Awards; won the Best International Actor award at the 2012 Irish Film And Television Awards; nominated for the Actor of the Year award at the 2012 London Critics Circle Film Awards; won the Best Actor in a Motion Picture award at the 2011 Satellite Awards and nominated for Choice Movie Actor: Drama award at the 2012 *Teen Choice* Awards.

In May 2012, a new issue of *Marie Claire* hit newsstands featuring an exclusive with Eva Mendes. In the interview, she talked about what it was like to shoot *The Place Beyond The Pines* with Ryan, saying, 'I have never felt so creatively satisfied on a film. He's amazing.' Pressed to acknowledge that he was her partner, she said, 'Stop, just stop. I'm not gonna budge. I feel uncomfortable talking about it. It's too personal.'

On 3 June 2012, the annual MTV Movie Awards ceremony was held at the Gibson Amphitheatre. Ryan had been nominated for Best Male Performance for his work on *Drive* (yet another accolade for that performance); Best Gut-Wrenching Performance, also for *Drive*, and Best Kiss, for the kiss he shared with Emma Stone in *Crazy, Stupid, Love*. As with the Golden Globes ceremony, he was not at the MTV Movie Awards. He had been seen leaving Los Angeles a day or so before, bound for Montreal, Canada, with Eva Mendes.

The reason he was heading for Canada was to attend his mother's graduation ceremony, which would take place on 6 June at Brock University, in St Catharines, Ontario. Donna Gosling was to graduate from teacher training studies. The audience was in disbelief that Ryan Gosling was in the audience, with Eva Mendes. He apparently jumped to his feet, clapping, when his mother's name was called out and she went to collect her diploma. But he did not want to upstage her in any way – a strong possibility since he had arrived with Mendes. When asked by a local newspaper for comment, he told them it was his mother's day and he had no further comment to make.

In July, following the aftermath of the cinema shooting in Aurora, Colorado, the first trailer for *Gangster Squad* – released in May – was taken down because it featured an excerpt from a scene in which a cinema audience is sprayed with machine-gun fire. A decision was made that this scene needed to be removed from the film and the narrative reshot to deal with its omission. Scheduled for release in September, the movie was put back to January 2013, giving Ruben Fleischer and crew time to shoot new scenes between 21 and 23 August 2012 before re-editing, as required.

At the start of September 2012, Ryan began work on a new movie by Terrence Malick, legendary director of films such as *Badlands*, *Days Of Heaven*, *The Thin Red Line* and *The Tree Of Life*. Late in 2011, the project had been announced under the title *Lawless*. The film, one of two the veteran filmmaker had written himself and was shooting back to back, would star Ryan and be filmed on location in Austin, Texas, and in the Yucatán region of Mexico. His co-stars would include Rooney Mara, Natalie Portman, Michael Fassbender, Christian Bale and Cate Blanchett.

Malick kept the plot under wraps. All that was known was that it was set among the music scene in Austin, Texas, with the story of two love triangles intersected. With more detail on the musical aspect of the film, the *Guardian* reported in March 2012 that Malick had been shooting at the Austin City Limits Music Festival in September 2011 and since then had also shot footage featuring Arcade Fire, Fleet Foxes and Neon Indian.

By then, Malick had given up on the title *Lawless* since The Weinstein Company wanted to use it for a Prohibition-era film by John Hillcoat that they were gearing up to release. Asked if he would mind them using the title, Malick, being an admirer of Hillcoat's work, gave up his claim and his own work became known as an untitled Terrence Malick film.

Malick had started pre-production in late 2011 and also had the principal actors trial out scenes together – which is how pictures of Ryan and Rooney Mara on set together had appeared on the internet in November 2011. In the photos, Ryan is pictured wearing a black leather jacket, black faded jeans and sunglasses, standing in one shot with his arm around Mara, with various shots of them lingering backstage at what looked to be a music festival.

In August 2012, it was announced that Ryan was putting together his directorial debut. Although he had talked about this before – *The Lord's Resistance* – it had slowly disappeared from being mentioned in interviews, this time he was actively assembling his cast and crew. As with *The Lord's Resistance*, he had once again written the screenplay, titling it *How To Catch A Monster*. More than that, he had already secured *Mad Men*'s Christina Hendricks to star as the single mother of two sons, one of them discovering a secret road leading to an underwater town.

To get the film made, Ryan also set up his own production company, Phantasma Films, to co-produce with Marc Platt Productions and Bold Films. This showed that he was becoming serious about ways to expand into the film industry beyond acting and seemed to indicate that he was intending, like George Clooney, to develop multiple avenues so that in the future he could be poised not only to act, but also to write, produce and direct his own features and, if he saw logic in it, to come in as producer. This multi-pronged expansion is a fairly standard Hollywood pattern that actors and actresses often follow when they have amassed enough of a personal fortune to have the financial muscle not only to be able to start acting in the films they want to make, but also to come into projects that interest them as co-producer.

On 7 September 2012, he was back in Canada for the premiere of *The Place Beyond The Pines* at the Toronto International Film Festival. The film screened at the Princess of Wales Theatre and, when Ryan arrived, he lingered on the red carpet, signing autographs for fans. Joining him were Derek Cianfrance, Eva Mendes and Bradley Cooper. Ryan was wearing a suit with a white shirt buttoned all the way up to the top, but no tie – a sartorial look favoured by David Lynch. In one photo from the event, he stands next to Eva, with Bradley Cooper to her right and the three appear to be sharing a joke.

Ryan made a flash appearance at a charity event at The Texas School For The Deaf on Saturday, 27 October. He was nearby filming the untitled Terrence Malick project and turned up unannounced with co-stars Rooney Mara and Michael Fassbender. The fundraising event, called the Spooky Skedaddle 5K, raised a total of $20,000. A news article in *The Washington Post* explained that some of the production crew trucks for the Malick film had been parked out on the campus of the school and the Spooky Skedaddle organisers had been hoping Ryan and the cast and crew might stray into the fundraiser and lend the day some hardcore celebrity appeal. As it happened, he helped boost funds raised by paying $50 for a $1 glow-in-the-dark cotton candy at a stall managed by a group of deaf children. He happily signed autographs for children at the event – proving as ever that, when it comes to kids, he will do anything to bring a smile to their faces.

Over the Thanksgiving weekend, Ryan took Eva to see Jessica Chastain appear in a play, *The Heiress*, at the Walter Kerr Theatre. They found their seats just before the performance started, in a bid to attend incognito, but were soon spotted by audience members and their outing ended up in the press.

In December that year, Ryan was photographed helping a deliveryman bring a consignment of home entertainment into his house. He had apparently bought speakers to enhance the sound quality of his home entertainment system. New stories about this mentioned that his home was in Studio City, Los Angeles – suggesting that he had once more set up home in Los Angeles, as well as in New York. It seemed he was at home as he had just finished shooting the Terrence Malick film and was enjoying some rare days off to unwind.

The New Year opened with the premiere of *Gangster Squad* on 7 January 2013 at Grauman's Chinese Theatre in Hollywood. Ryan turned up wearing a brown three-piece suit, a white shirt and a black tie. As was often the case, he attended the premiere with his mother, Donna. Much was made of her outfit – she had told reporters she had borrowed clothes from Eva Mendes. Donna was quoted by the *E* channel: 'I'm wearing Eva Mendes – she let me raid her closet.' Interestingly, Ryan was also quoted as saying, 'My mother's wearing all my girlfriend's clothes.' This was the first time that he had actually referred to Eva as his girlfriend in a public context and, given the degree to which he usually keeps his private life strictly private, it suggests that he was feeling more serious about Eva than about any previous girlfriend.

To promote *Gangster Squad*, he appeared on *Jimmy Kimmel Live!* on 9 January. Aside from sitting for an interview, he also appeared in a wacky skit with Will Ferrell, in which they were the 'Knife Guys'. This involved Ferrell opening the skit, essentially a TV shopping spoof, by mock arguing with Jimmy Kimmel about how the Knife Guys were meant to be on TV at this time and not Kimmel. After Ferrell finished demonstrating the merits of a large Samurai sword, Kimmel asked if he was finished. Ferrell said that he had not finished and had far more to cover in his slot. He added that he wanted to bring out a guest called Ryan, and out came Gosling to the hysterical response of the audience. Wearing safety goggles and holding the kind of strap-on tray that ice-cream vendors tend to wear at events, Ryan did little more than mug for the applause until he too joined in the mock argument with Kimmel, telling him that he was not meant to be on air – only the Knife Guys. Ferrell then proceeded to hack at the goodies on Ryan's tray with the Samurai sword, while Ryan did his best to try to stifle laughter. At the end of the skit, Ferrell pretended to injure himself with the knife and grimaced and winced as he clutched his hand, while Kimmel looked on, expressing mock concern. Ryan kept shaking his head, playing along with the mock argument.

A week later, on 13 January, *Gangster Squad* opened at cinemas amid a wave of tepid reviews. For *The New York Times*, the film was 'less a movie than a costume party run amok', while *USA Today* believed it constituted 'a lurid and ludicrous Mob thriller that glorifies a gangland lifestyle'. Despite this underwhelming critical reception, the movie took $17,070,347 over the opening weekend and went on to gross $105,200,903 worldwide.

At the turn of February, it was revealed that Ryan had cast his partner, Eva Mendes, in *How To Catch A Monster*. She would play a character called Cat, who was part of a gang. Also attached to the project were New York-born, Irish-raised actress Saoirse Ronan, whose credits include *The Lovely Bones*, *Atonement*, *Hanna* and *Violet and Daisy*; British actor Matt Smith, best known for playing The Doctor in the revamped *Dr Who* TV series between 2010 and 2013; and Ben Mendelsohn, the Polish-Australian actor who has appeared in films such as *Trespass*, *Killing Them Softly* and *The Dark Knight Rises*.

After the premiere at the Toronto International Film Festival, *The Place Beyond The Pines* next screened at the Glasgow Film Festival on both 23 and 24 February – the first of two screenings marking the film's European premiere – before opening the Discovery Zone Film Festival in Luxembourg on 28 February. With this film, plus *Only God Forgives* and the upcoming Terrence Malick movie in the pipeline, Ryan would now focus on making *How To Catch A Monster* – causing fans to wonder what this would mean for his acting career.

EPILOGUE

In March 2013, in an interview with *The Hollywood Reporter*, Ryan let slip that, for the time being, he was planning to focus on directing and to take a break from acting. Of his recent season of non-stop acting, he said, 'I think I've kind of over-saturated myself with myself, made a lot of movies and have lost a little perspective on what I'm doing so this is a way for me to still make a film but have a new experience doing it and see it from another perspective, which I think I need right now.'

His comments immediately went viral and caused panic among fans, who feared this spelled another protracted interlude where their favourite actor would step away to focus on another kind of work, as he had done before. In response to the panic, British movie rental and streaming company Blinkbox set up a helpline – The Gosline – which fans could dial for solace, where they'd be met by Ryan saying cleverly selected lines from *The Notebook*, creating the effect that he appeared to be soothing their sadness over his decision to take a break and re-think where his acting career was heading.

On 28 March, *The Place Beyond The Pines* premiered at the Landmark Sunshine cinema in New York. Ryan and Eva Mendes were both present. This time he was wearing a dark velvet Gucci suit, dark tie and a white shirt; Mendes wore a peach-coloured Prada dress. According to the Red Carpet Fashion Awards, who were wowed by his ensemble, Ryan doesn't employ a stylist to help him dress for public appearances. While posing for photographs on the red carpet, he made a point of calming fears that he might be leaving acting for a very long time. He told the press that he was merely taking a break so that he could concentrate on directing *How To Catch A Monster* – 'I should have been more clear; I'm just taking a break to direct. I'm sorry about that.'

On 31 March 2013, the film opened in US cinemas, taking $279,457 across the opening weekend. The *Guardian* praised Ryan's performance, saying, 'Gosling gives his most open and engaging performance yet, his sleepy, woozy mannerisms developing into a complex interior world of hurt, resentment and disappointment'; as did *The New York Times*, who observed, 'Mr. Gosling's cool self-possession – the only thing he was allowed to display in *Drive* – is complicated, made interesting by hints of childlike innocence and vulnerability.'

With another of his films released, Ryan was finalising details of *How To Catch A Monster* ahead of May 2013, when filming was set to begin. Incredibly, he was still only 32. With so much achieved in such a short time, the actor finds himself in an enviable position whereby he has achieved movie-star status without compromising a dot of critical acclaim. And, to get to this point, he has shown a canny knack for exiting a corner whenever he sees one on the horizon. This meant breaking out of children's TV when he saw it starting to become what would likely be a short-lived career; leaving Canada for Los Angeles to swap kids' TV parts for film roles; taking the romantic lead in *The Notebook* just as he was beginning to become typecast as an actor who plays offbeat, troubled, detached characters; working as a sandwich maker when he realised Hollywood was tightening its grip; taking an intense role as that drug-abusing teacher in *Half Nelson* when he was about to find himself typecast as a pin-up romantic lead following the success of *The Notebook*; pouring his creativity into making music when he wanted to refresh and take his acting talents to the next level; gambling his reputation on a mainstream comic turn in *Crazy, Stupid, Love*; and forming collaborative recurring relationships with the directors Nicolas Winding Refn and Derek Cianfrance when he was eager to challenge himself within the creative shorthand of an existing relationship. Finally, after the box-office triumph that came with *Crazy, Stupid, Love* and critical kudos heaped on his work in *The Ides Of March* and *Drive*, Ryan could turn his ever-ambitious, restless energy towards fulfilling the dream of writing and directing his own film – a yearning that began with the aborted *Lord's Resistance* screenplay and would now be realised in *How To Catch A Monster*.

Aside from the widespread interest that naturally surrounds

How To Catch A Monster, wherever Ryan Gosling's career heads in the coming years, it's a given that integrity will be to the fore and he will tackle every project with his trademark all-consuming, total-immersion approach. One also senses that, personally, he will settle down soon and take his bachelor status off the market.

And not too far off in the future, he will, of course, win that Best Actor award at the Oscars and, who knows, maybe even Best Screenplay and Best Director, too, at some point. Regardless of how all this plays out, he will no doubt continue to be seen taking the Haunted Mansion ride at Disneyland, reconnecting with that 12-year-old boy who would wander round Disney World, daydreaming inside the lucky break he'd suddenly conjured up for himself.

FILMOGRAPHY

AS ACTOR

2014: Untitled Terrence Malick Project
Directed by: Terrence Malick
Cast: Rooney Mara, Natalie Portman, Michael Fassbender, Christian Bale

2013: *Only God Forgives* (as Julian)
Directed by: Nicolas Winding Refn
Cast: Kristin Scott Thomas, Tom Burke, Yayaying, Vithaya Pansringarm

2013: *Gangster Squad* (as Sgt. Jerry Wooters)
Directed by: Ruben Fleischer
Cast: Sean Penn, Holt McCallany, Wade Williams, James Landry Hébert, Ambyr Childers, Josh Brolin, Emma Stone

2012: *The Place Beyond The Pines* (as Luke)
Directed by: Derek Cianfrance
Cast: Bradley Cooper, Eva Mendes, Ray Liotta, Rose Byrne

2011: *Drunk History Christmas* (as Pa)
Directed by: Derek Waters, Jeremy Konner
Cast: Jim Carrey, Eva Mendes, Allan McLeod

2011: *The Ides Of March* (as Stephen Meyers)
Directed by: George Clooney
Cast: George Clooney, Paul Giamatti, Philip Seymour Hoffman, Evan Rachel Wood, Marisa Tomei

2011: *Crazy, Stupid, Love* (as Jacob Palmer)
Directed by: Glenn Ficarra, John Requa
Cast: Steve Carell, Julianne Moore, Emma Stone, Kevin Bacon, Marisa Tomei

2011: *Drive* (as Driver)
Directed by: Nicolas Winding Refn
Cast: Carey Mulligan, Albert Brooks, Christina Hendricks

2010: *Blue Valentine* (as Dean)
Directed by: Derek Cianfrance
Cast: Michelle Williams, Faith Wladyka

2010: *All Good Things* (as David Marks)
Directed by: Andrew Jarecki
Cast: Kirsten Dunst, Frank Langella, Kristen Wiig, Lily Rabe

2010: *ReGeneration* (Narration)
Directed by: Phillip Montgomery
Cast: Noam Chomsky, Talib Kweli

2007: *Lars And The Real Girl* (as Lars Lindstrom)
Directed by: Craig Gillespie
Cast: Emily Mortimer, Paul Schneider, Patricia Clarkson

2007 *Fracture* (as Willy Beachum)
Directed by: Gregory Hoblit
Cast: Anthony Hopkins, David Strathairn, Rosamund Pike, Embeth Davidtz

2006: *Half Nelson* (as Dan Dunne)
Directed by: Ryan Fleck
Cast: Shareeka Epps, Anthony Mackie

2005: *Stay* (as Henry Letham)
Directed by: Marc Forster
Cast: Ewan McGregor, Naomi Watts, Bob Hoskins, Janeane Garofalo

2005: *I'm Still Here: Real Diaries Of Young People Who Lived During The Holocaust* (voice of Ilya Gerber)
Directed by: Lauren Lazin
Cast: Kate Hudson, Brittany Murphy, Amber Tamblyn, Elijah Wood, Zach Braff

2004: *The Notebook* (as Noah)
Directed by: Nick Cassavetes
Cast: Rachel McAdams, Gena Rowlands, James Garner, Sam Shepard

2003: *The United States Of Leland* (as Leland P. Fitzgerald)
Directed by: Matthew Ryan Hoge
Cast: Don Cheadle, Michelle Williams, Chris Klein, Jena Malone, Kevin Spacey, Lena Olin, Sherilyn Fenn, Ann Magnuson, Martin Donovan

2002: *Murder By Numbers* (as Richard Haywood)
Directed by: Barbet Schroeder
Cast: Sandra Bullock, Ben Chaplin, Michael Pitt, Chris Penn, Agnes Bruckner

2002: *The Slaughter Rule* (as Roy Chutney)
Directed by: Alex Smith, Andrew J. Smith
Cast: David Morse, Clea DuVall, Kelly Lynch

2001: *The Believer* (as Danny Balint)
Directed by: Henry Bean
Cast: Billy Zane, Theresa Russell, Summer Phoenix, Elizabeth Reaser

2000: *Remember The Titans* (as Alan Bosley)
Directed by: Boaz Yakin
Cast: Denzel Washington, Will Patton, Kate Bosworth

TV ROLES

1998–99: *Young Hercules* (as Hercules)

1999: *Hercules: The Legendary Journeys* (as Zylus)

1999: *The Unbelievables* (as Josh)

1997–98: *Breaker High* (as Sean Hanlon)

1998: *Nothing Too Good For A Cowboy* (as Tommy)

1997: *Frankenstein And Me* (as Kenny)

1996: *PSI Factor: Chronicles Of The Paranormal* (as Adam in episode 'Dream House/UFO Encounter')

1996: *Kung Fu: The Legend Continues* (as Kevin in episode 'Dragon's Lair')

1996: *Road To Avonlea* (as Bret McNulty in episode 'From Away')

1996: *Goosebumps* (as Greg Banks in episode 'Say Cheese And Die')

1996: *Flash Forward* (as Scott Stuckey in episodes 'Double Bill' and 'Skate Bait')

1996: *The Adventures Of Shirley Holmes* (as Sean in episode 'The Case Of The Burning Building')

1996: *Ready Or Not* (as Matt Kalinsky in episode 'I Do, I Don't')

1995: *Are You Afraid Of The Dark?* (as Jamie Leary in episode 'The Tale Of Station 109.1')

AS PRODUCER

2014: *How To Catch A Monster*
2010: *ReGeneration*
2010: *Blue Valentine*

AS DIRECTOR

2014: *How To Catch A Monster*

AS WRITER

2014: *How To Catch A Monster*